BUILD YOUR FORTUNE WITH ONLINE STORE

OR

ESSENTIAL GUIDE TO PRESTASHOP

New York

2014

©2014 Copyright by Roman Lytvyn

All rights reserved. This book or any portion thereof may not be reproduced or used in any manner whatsoever without the express written permission of the publisher except for the use of brief quotations in a book review or scholarly journal. This book is written as a personal recommendation and doesn't guarantee any good results or success in online business. All examples are from personal experiences of the author. All other materials used in this book are property of their legal owners and are protected by their owners' rights. All similarities are by coincidence only. Book was written from thoughts of the author.

First Printing: 2014

ISBN #: 978-1-312-42819-5
Content ID: 15090074

800BP
1967 Ocean Ave #1C
Brooklyn, NY, 11230

USA

www.800bp.com

sales@800bp.com

DEDICATION

To my lovely wife and family, who were always there for me.

Thank you for believing in me!

Without your help, support and patience, I would never achieve my dream.

CONTENTS

1. ONLINE BUSINESS INTRODUCTION

2. HOSTING, DOMAIN AND INSTALLATION

3. SETUP AND COMMON PREFERENCES

4. CHANGING A TEMPLATE

5. SHIPPING, TAXES AND LOCALIZATION

6. PAYMENTS PROCESSING

7. ADDING PRODUCTS AND CATEGORIES

8. ORDERS PROCESSING

9. MODULES

10. SOCIAL NETWORKS IMPLEMENTATION

11. STATISTICS AND EMPLOYEE MANAGEMENT

12. SEO FOR YOUR STORE

13. FINAL TOUCH UP'S AND UPGRADES

1
ONLINE BUSINESS INTRODUCTION

You have a business idea, but you don't know how to make it work?

You want to sell online, but you can't afford a programmer? That's exactly what I've been through.

However, later I decided that I'm not worse than others, and I can do it myself.

I spent many hours learning and trying, and then I realized that it is very easy. All you need is just a proper explanation and training and you can use your Prestashop online store within 15 minutes and you can start making money right away.

So let's get started.

Let's assume that you have a boutique or an electronic store and you are not  visible online. Today 80% of your potential customers are looking for you on the internet on their phones, tablets or computers. How is it done? Easy. They open a map and type, for example: "electronics", and get different addresses of stores but you are not there – you're losing money!

Let's assume that you are on the map, but you don't have a website – 70% of people, that are looking for a specific item, will open your neighbor's website and buy from them directly.

Let's assume that you are on the map and that you have a website. BUT! You forgot one extremely important detail – user-friendly interface.

Yes! Your potential customers will leave your website if they find it hard to navigate or slow loading. You have actually 4 seconds from where your website loaded to the point, that your customer would find something interesting and keep browsing your store.

Only 4 seconds to get attention of your customer. That's why you need a website that will look professional, user friendly, secure and that will load fast. All this you can achieve with prestashop.

Now let's assume that you have no store and no products at all. You are a  housewife without a job, you have hundreds of things to do in the kitchen, you can't leave your kids alone at home, but you have a computer with Internet access and 2 hours a day of free time while your kids are asleep. I tell you what - You are a potential millionaire and you don't know about it. You can make lots of money with your online store even if you don't have what to sell. All you need is to find a dropship supplier.

Yes, there are companies out there that will do all the dirty shipping work for you. Just register with one of the companies that process dropship orders and you are ready to make money with your online store. You don't need to stack up products in your basement, you don't need to pack them and go to the post office to send them to your customers. Most importantly, you don't need to buy any products upfront. You spend $0 and that gives you 0% of risk. You can make money without spending a dime. After you get an order on your online store, just buy this item from your dropshipper for much lower price than you sell, and they will ship it directly to your customer. Moreover, they will include invoice with your logo and info for your customers. That way your customers will still think that you have sent them this order, not dealer. All the profit from this sale goes directly to you. For example: You sold a pair of pants for $50 and those same pants cost you $10. When customer buys them from your online store, he/she pays $50 to you, and you are buying from a dropshipper and pay $10 to a dropshipper for the same pair of pants. That way you have $40 of clean profit after few mouse clicks.

Two thirds of Americans are shopping online. And about 70% of them saying that online shopping is more convenient for them, and it saves them time and money. 43% of internet users are frustrated by the lack of information they encounter while using internet to buy goods. More people would shop online if they trusted e-commerce environment. And that's what your customers are looking for – easy looking but complete description, secure feeling and fast loading.

Whether you want to sell clothing or electronics, cosmetics or games for download, you can do it all with prestashop online store. You will ask what prestashop is. Is it a programming language or is it some kind of a company that you need to pay every month? NO!

Prestashop is a free and open source content management system (CMS), in other words, it's a program through which you can create and run your e-commerce online store website, without having any special programming skills or knowledge of any programming coding. Thanks to this, prestashop have become one of the most popular CMS and, as it is an open source, it gives programmers the ability to build 3rd party modules with fully customizable features. Prestashop also have awesome security features, which make it safe and reliable.

A very important feature of prestashop is a merchandizing solution - full range of options to have all your products, customers and invoices in one place, as well as automatic order processing and discounts/promotion integrations. Prestashop also gives you ability to choose your employees' rights and see all the statistics about your online store.

So bottom line - Prestashop.

-It is free

-It is fully customizable

-It is easy to use

-It gives us an ability to create professional online store without coding

-It is secure and reliable software with proven results.

-It gives us full range of merchandizing solutions needed for any business

-It helps us find correct marketing solution for our business using statistics results.

-It is search engines friendly

-It is fast

It's time to start your online store and install Prestashop!

2
HOSTING, DOMAINS AND INSTALLATION

Before starting let me explain you few things about domains.

Most of your potential customers will not remember domain address with more than 3 words. Best way, of course, would be a one word address, but today with all that internet popularity it is really hard to find simple yet correct domain name for your store containing one word. It is much easier to find a 2-3 words address and sometimes that would be your best bet. For example, if you have an electronic store in Brooklyn, try to use your location in your domain address, for example - NYCElectronics.com - that way you will be able to stand out in your specific area and will possibly get more customers in your physical location and more customers from your region.

However, internet is such an amazing thing that gives you an ability to sell all over the world, while you are on the island drinking margarita and enjoying a sunset with your other half. No matter what domain name you choose, you will always be able to use SEO techniques to promote your store with organic search phrases (see: SEO Chapter).

I recommend using your company name or as alternative - simple, easy to remember phrases for your domain address. Most of the time you can buy your domain name together with your hosting. In case that your hosting provider doesn't have this feature, you can always buy a domain from any popular registrar such as hostgator.com, justhost.com, godaddy.com etc.

After buying your domain from a different registrar than your hosting provider, you need to change nameservers on your domain to point to your hosting account where you will have your online store website stored.

It is not that hard as it sounds. You need to get nameservers attributes from your hosting provider and paste them into your domain preferences. You can always ask your domain/hosting support team and they will set it up for you.

If you're buying your domain with hosting, it will automatically be preset, and you don't need to change that.

Today it doesn't matter if you buy .com, .org, .net or any other extension. Your website will still be popular and visible thanks to metatags, description and organic search terms of your products (See: SEO Chapter). However, to give an impression of a big company I recommend ".com" as your online web address.

Shopping for hosting is a little different story.

First of all, you need to check which company gives you more space, bandwitch and options. Some companies have more of one and lack of the other. Depending on the website you are trying to build, you need to know what your needs are. For example, if you're looking to build an informational website without selling features, where you will have info about you and your company, address and contact form page you don't need anything powerful, as those type of websites need very small amount of space and resources. However, if you are trying to build an online store, where you can have thousands of products (each product have separate page), you need it to be fast enough to get your visitor's attention in the first 4 seconds, as I mentioned before. That's when you need to get a better hosting account.

I recommend hostgator.com as your hosting account provider. They offer unlimited disc space and unlimited bandwidth in any of their plans. For informational websites without selling features I recommend their "HATCHLING" or "BABY" plans, but for e-commerce online store I recommend their "BUSINESS" plan. That is just my opinion as an author of this book, you are not required to buy hosting or domains directly from that company. Here is a list of other popular hosting providers I recommend:

GoDaddy.com

HostGator.com

JustHost.com

Register.com

Web.com

BlueHost.com

iPage.com

Etc.

When buying hosting for online store website, you need to be sure that you will have a cPanel for easy navigation, as well as a private SSL and IP Address for security and speed. Business account from "hostgator" gives you all these for free and one more interesting feature that comes with this plan is a Toll Free number with 100 free minutes included. If you plan to build an online store, it will be a big plus for your business, when your customers can call you to get some additional information about products you sell. You can always use your phone number instead, but a Toll Free number will give your customers this safe "Big Company" feeling.

Cpanel In your hosting account is a control panel. You can open it by typing http://yourdomainname/cpanel

Enter your Login and Password and your cPanel will load.

What can you do with it? That is your hosting and website control.

First of all, you can create your own professional extension email address for example: info@yourdomainname.com. This way your company will look even more professional and reliable.

Moreover, you can manage your web settings, as well as all your files can be managed through "filemanager" from cPanel. You can create your databases, manage security options, check website statistics and, of course, you can install programs to your hosting account - All this and much more from your cPanel.

I will not explain all cPanel functions here, but will stop on few.

There are lots of programs available to install to your hosting server through "Fantastico" and "Quick Installs".

Also, you will often use "filemanager" for your ftp uploads and Email client, in case you create your professional email account.

It is also important for every business to know where your customers are coming from, which advertisement works best and how customers are getting around your store. Those questions can be answered through your "AWStatistics" icon.

You can also find your dedicated IP address on the bottom left corner of your cPanel. "Inodes" (total amount of files on your storage hosting) and space limits info can be found there as well.

To get started with online store you need to have SSL connection, and that can be obtained from your cPanel too. (See Payment Chapter for more details)

INSTALLATION

There are few different ways to install Prestashop. I will explain here the most common one. Prestashop is a CMS that can be installed only online or on a local server. We will install it on our Hostgator account. There are 2 most popular ways to install prestashop.

Installation Example #1

Firstly, you need to login to your hosting account cPanel by typing http://www.YourDomainName.com/cpanel in your browser.

Type in your login and password and press Enter to login.

Scroll down to Software/Services and open QuickInstall.

That's the place where the most popular CMS can be installed to your server.

On your left side locate Prestashop and click on its icon.

Confirm your choice by pressing "continue".

In the installation window from the scroll down menu you need to choose a domain name, on which it will be installed.

(Also you can install it into some folder, if you want to practice first. You can type folder name in the field after domain name. And later move it to your root folder. However, I don't recommend this, as after you move it to your root folder, you will need to reset all modules again.)

You can Enable Auto Upgrades by putting a checkmark next to it.

Type your email address, desired site title, first and last name and press "Install Now"!

(Make sure your email address is correct, as you will use it to login to your back office later.)

Wait until your Prestashop is installed.

To enter Admin Section, you will need to copy password and press on the link that appears. Press on Index.php to access Login page.

Enter email address that you used during installation and paste password that you copied after installation was done.

Index of /admin-1401991504

- Parent Directory
- ajax-tab.php
- ajax.php
- ajax_products_list.php
- ajaxfilemanager/
- autoupgrade/
- backup.php
- cron_currency_rates.php
- displayImage.php
- drawer.php
- footer.inc.php
- functions.php
- get-file-admin.php
- grider.php
- header.inc.php
- index.php
- init.php
- login.php
- password.php
- pdf.php
- searchcron.php
- themes/
- uploadProductFile.php
- uploadProductFileAttribute.php

Apache Server at obenterprise.com Port 80

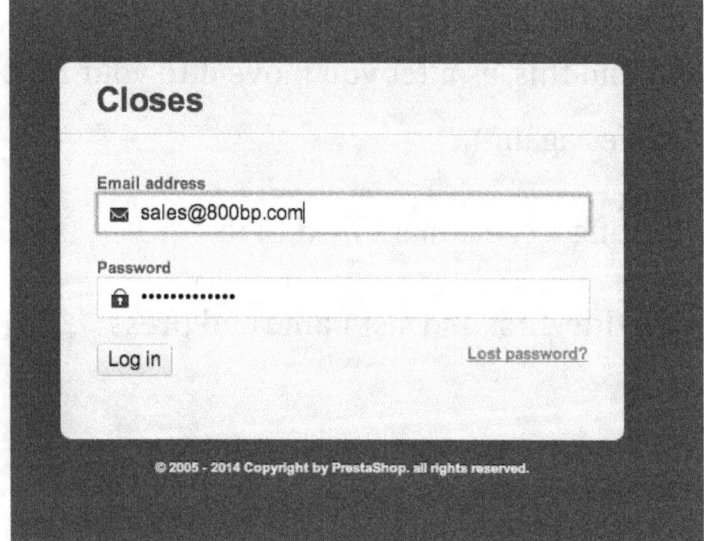

Press "login" to enter backoffice of your prestashop.

I recommend changing your password right after the installation by going to "My Preferences".

Enter New Password and press "Save".

Your Prestashop is installed and ready to use.

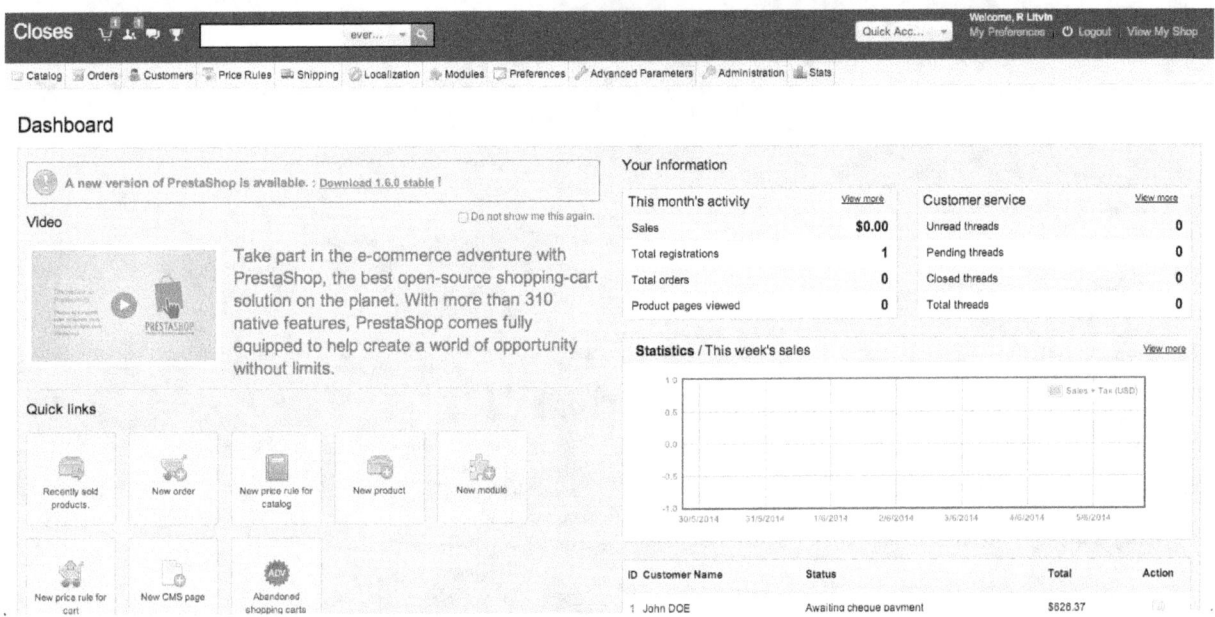

If you press "View My Shop" on the right side of your screen it will open your website. Very often you need to edit your (.htaccess) file, which is located in your root section. Open "File Manager" from your cPanel.

Open folder containing your website and locate (.htaccess) file.

Press on it and choose Code Editor on the top of your File Manager window.

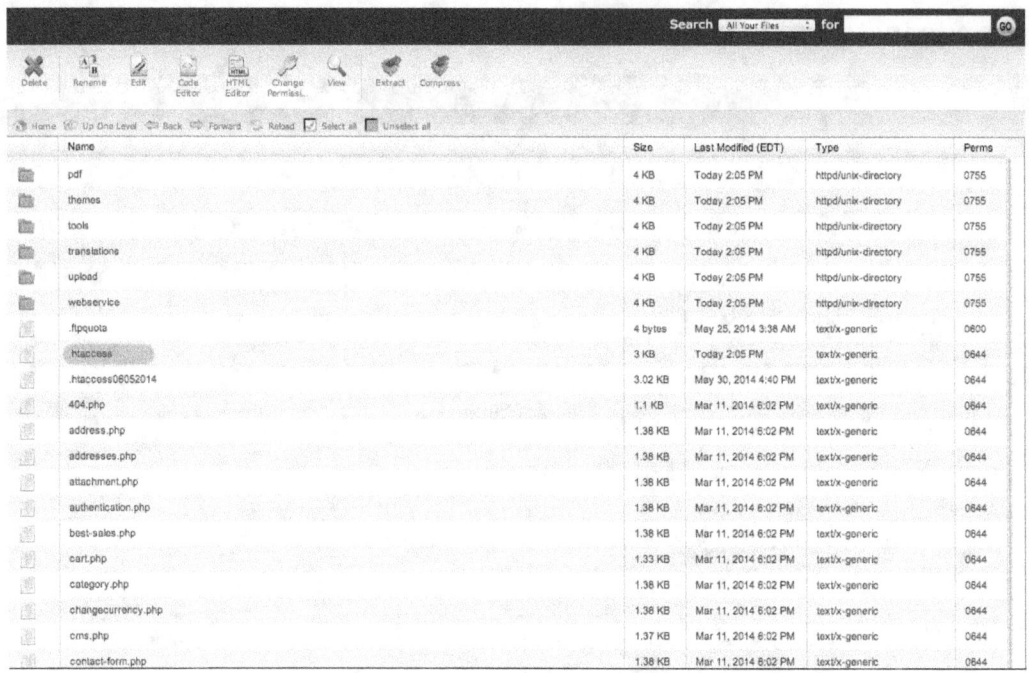

Enter this path

DirectoryIndex index.php On the very top of the file. Press "Save".

Now Your front office website will load correctly.

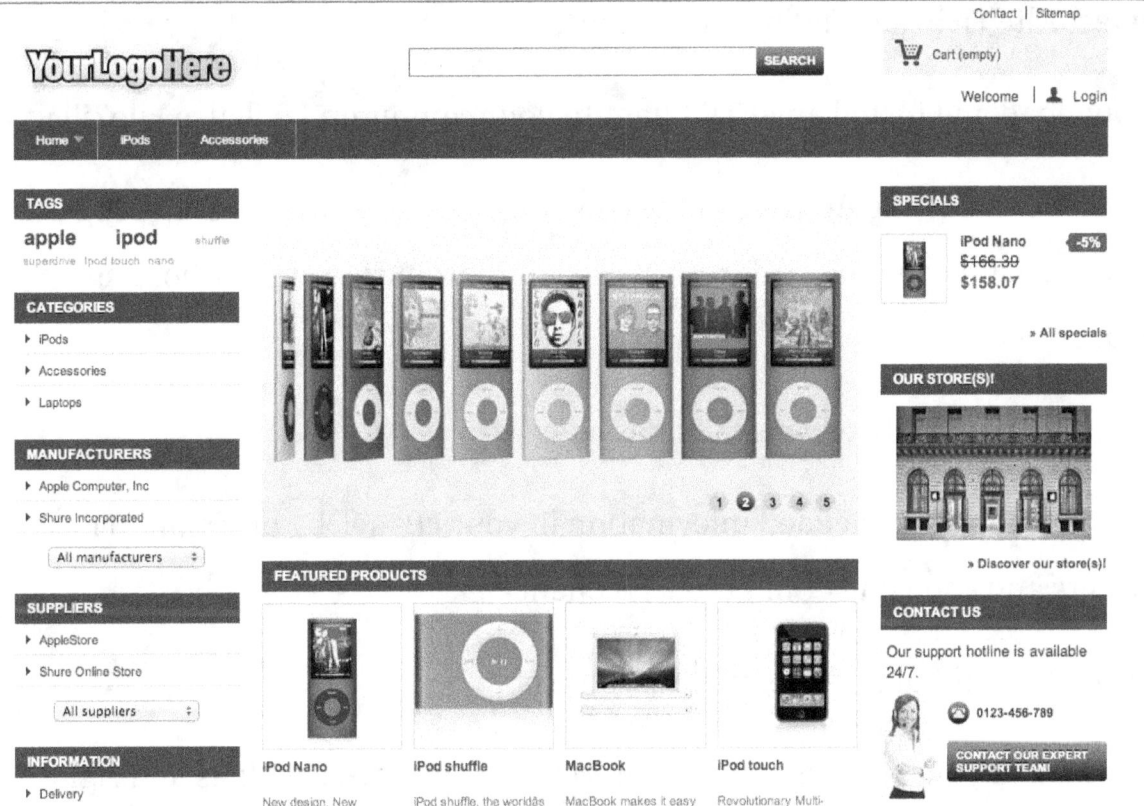

Congratulation! You have just installed Prestashop to your hosting account.

Installation Example #2

1. Go to official Prestashop website.

http://www.prestashop.com and click "download prestashop".

2. Unzip files to your computer.

3. Login to your cPanel on your hosting account by typing http://www.YourDomainName.com/cpanel in your browser.

4. Scroll down to locate My SQL Database Wizard.

5. Enter database name and then press "Next".

6. Create a password and press "Create User".

7. Select All Privileges and press "Create".

8. Download and install any FTP Client to your computer. I will use FileZilla.

9. Enter your Hosting Address at the top of the page in your FileZilla program (you can locate your Host Address at the left bottom side of your hosting account).

10. Enter your FTP Username and password.

(You can locate your needed information in your cPanel, by pressing FTP Accounts and choosing Configure FTP Client).

11. Press "QuickConnect" to process connection.

12. Locate all your Prestashop Files on your computer, select files and right click on them, then choose "UPLOAD".

(It may take some time for the files to be transferred to your FTP.)

13. When all files were successfully uploaded, open your browser to install prestashop.

Enter http://www.yourdomainname.com/install

14. Choose the language you want to use to install prestashop in.

15. Accept License Terms & Conditions and press "Next".

16. Enter your information, email address and password which you want to use to enter into your Prestashop back office and press "Next".

17. Enter your database credentials, that you have created in earlier steps (name, username and password), and press "Test Your database Connection". If it was connected successfully press "Next".

18. Wait for the installation to be finished.

19. Delete your "install" folder from your host account through FileZilla or by opening filemanager from your cPanel.

20. Your installation is complete and you can start using your prestashop.

You might need to do changes to your .htaccess file as described in installation Example#1

Those are two most common and popular ways to install prestshop.

Other CMS's like Drupal, Joomla, Opencart etc. are installed same way with only few other changes.

3

SETUP AND COMMON PREFERENCES

After you installed prestashop, you need to do few simple changes in your settings.

You can access settings from your dashboard menu.

Click "Preferences" ->"General" and choose your main shop activity.

You can also enable SSL in this setting. I will mention it later in Payments Setup Chapter.

Click "Preferences"-> "Orders" and select which store checkout you wish to have for your customers: One Step Checkout or five steps standard buying process.

You can also allow gift wrapping and multi-shipping in this section.

Choose CMS page that you want your customers to accept, when they shop in your online store. By default it is Terms and Conditions page.

Click "Preferences"->"Products".

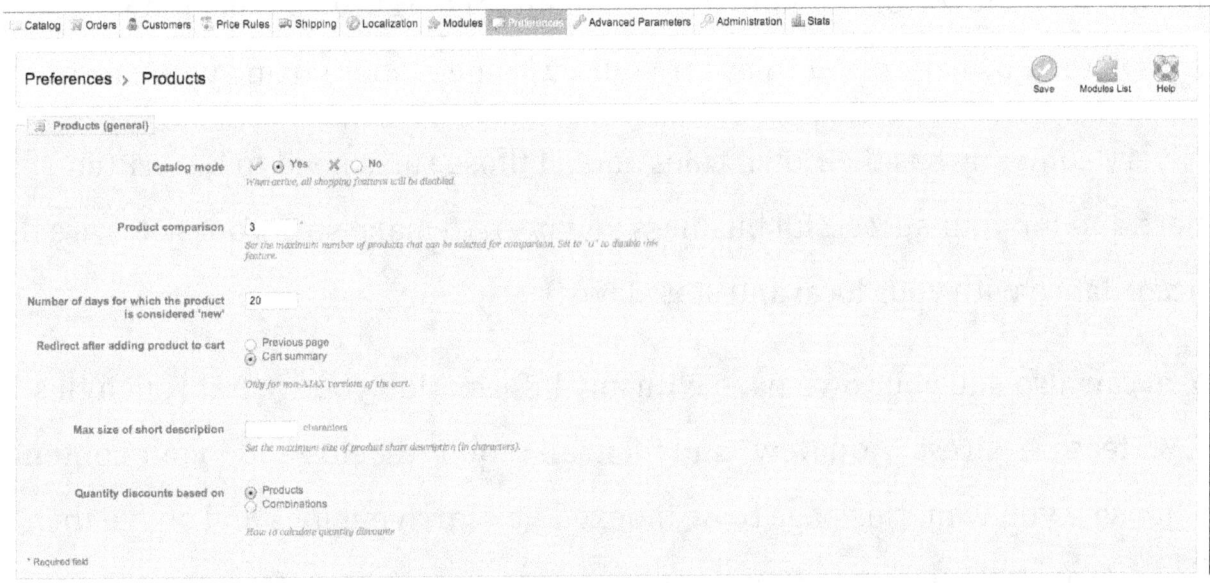

You can allow "Catalog Mode" – All your products will show up without possibility to buy.

And you can allow ordering of out of stock items.

In the "Preferences" tab you can also customize your "Store Contacts", "Search Options" and Geolocation of your customers.

Click "Preferences"->"Maintenance" to put your store in maintenance mode while you make changes. Press "ADD MY IP" to see changes in your front office. ATTENTION! Only you will be able to see changes, if your store is in maintenance mode. Your Customer will not be able to browse your website until you choose "Enable Shop".

Click "Preferences"->"Theme" to upload your Logo and switch between themes. I will show you how to change your theme in the next chapter.

Click "Preferences"->"CMS". Here you can type all your legal documentation information like: Terms and Condition of Use, Privacy Policy, Delivery, Payment and few words about your company. Make sure you include complete information and rules for your customers about using your store.

(Every company has their own rules and all those rules need to be written here and for your successful business you need to make sure your rules are in accordance with your local and state laws.)

You can also add your own page with any information you wish through this CMS feature. Press "Add New" and fill in all required fields - add your content. Choose if you want this page to be indexed by search engines and active then press "Save". Your customized page is ready.

You can add extra CMS category for faster access.

Click "Preferences"->"Images".

Change name, width and height of your images according to your theme documentation or leave it as they appear by default.

After making any changes in this field you need to scroll down and press "Regenerate thumbnails for all existing images".

For SEO Section will have a separate Chapter.

Performance of your store should always be adjusted due to theme settings.

Click "Advanced Preferences"-> Performance.

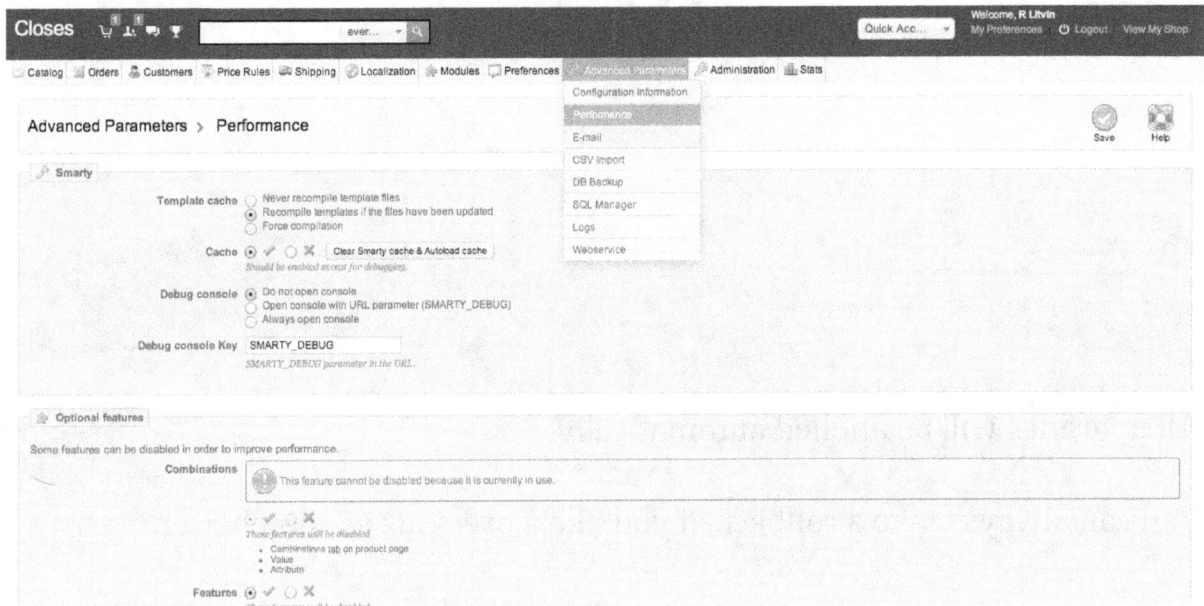

Check Use CCC for CSS & Use CCC for Java to reduce the loading time of your pages.

Also, after you have done some big changes to your store, it is recommended to "Clear Cash".

Click "Advanced Preferences"->"DB Backup" to process a manual backup of your store.

Your prestashop setup is complete and ready.

IF YOUR PRESTASHOP IS AN OLD VERSION, YOU CAN UPGRADE IT FROM YOUR BACK OFFICE. Click "Modules"-> One click Upgrade and press "Install" next to it. Check "Click here to put your shop under maintenance" And press "Upgrade prestashop now".

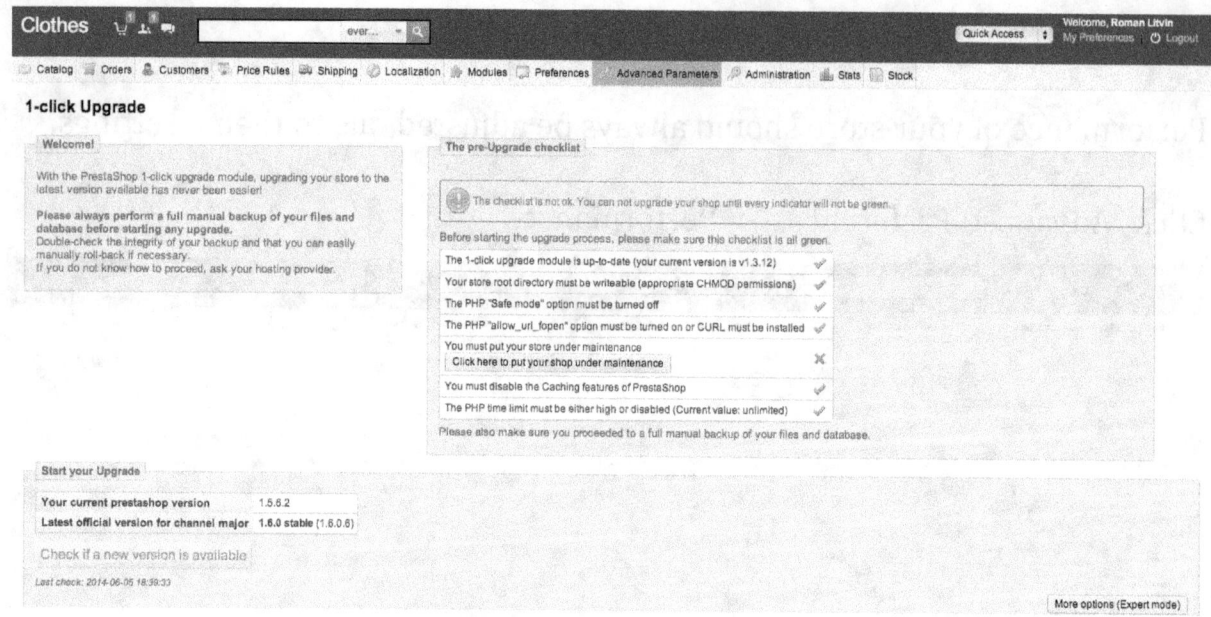

All upgrades will be applied automatically.

You can always make a rollback, if you like a previous version better.

4
CHANGING A TEMPLATE

A standard template is not what we are always looking for. Very often we need to have something more personalized for our store, and we want to be different than others. I recommend using approved sources for purchasing a template for your prestashop store. You can find lots of free templates online but, if you want something special, you can always purchase templates. I recommend http://themeforest.net for your template shopping. It's easy, reliable and affordable way to make your store look awesome. Make sure you choose prestashop from the menu when are looking for new themes. You need to be registered on their website to buy themes. Registration takes just a minute and you will have your theme downloaded to your computer.

To install a theme to your online shop you need to login to your back office.

Open the tab "Modules" and scroll down to "Import/Export a Theme" module.

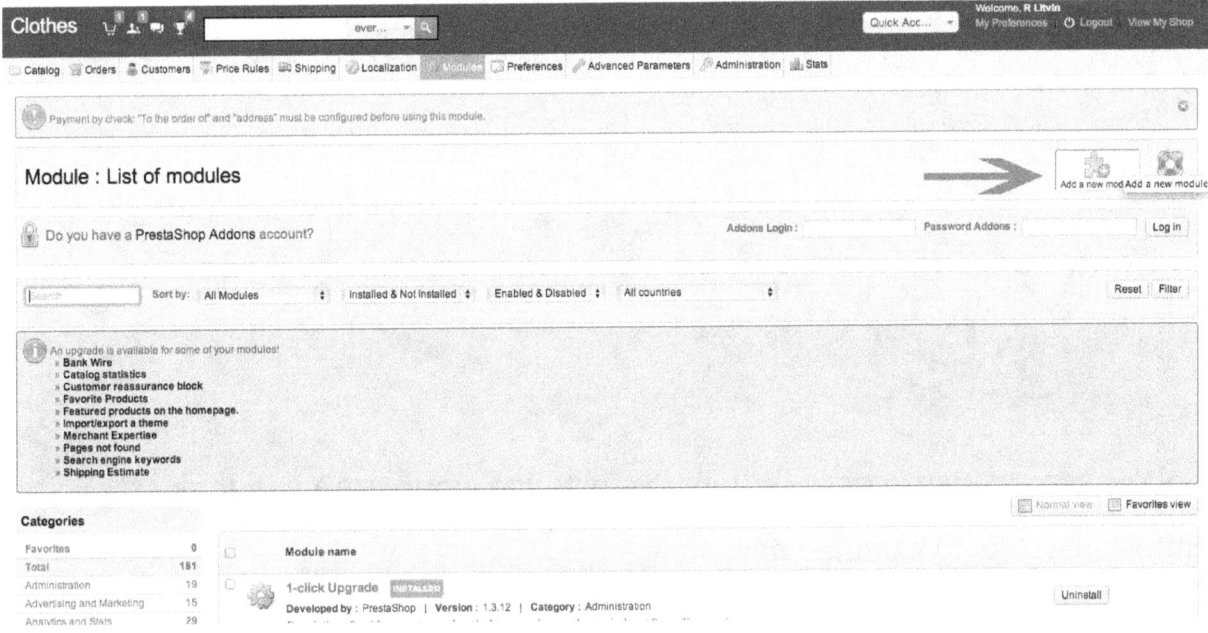

Press "Configure".

Choose .zip file that you have downloaded from http://themeforest.net to your computer and press "Next".

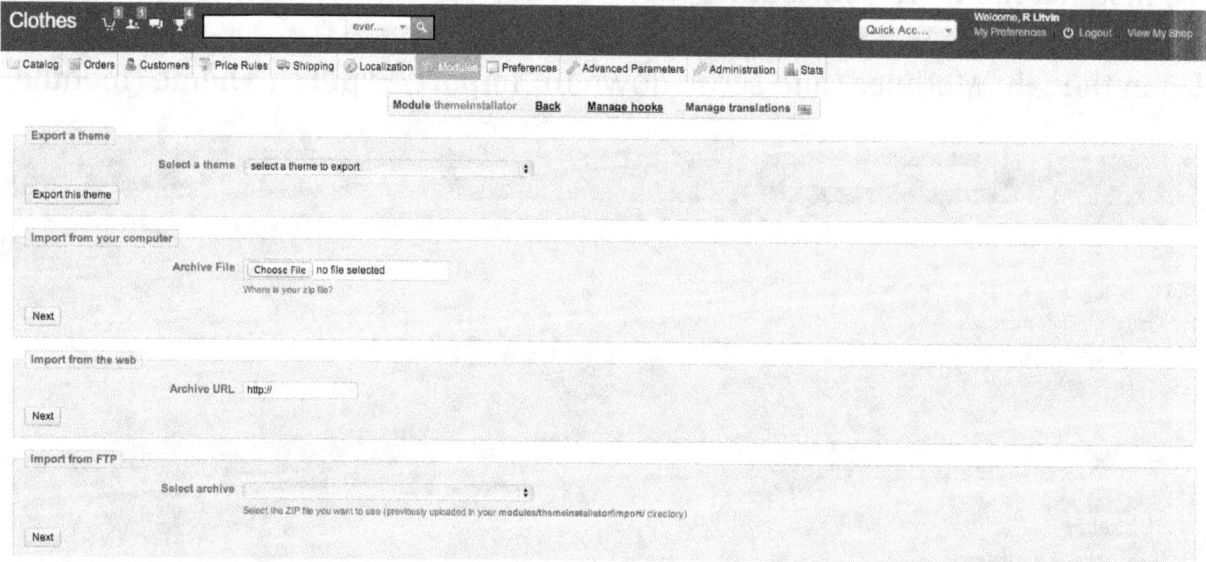

Follow screen instructions. When it is installed, your store will look differently, like in example below.

You need to check documentation of the exact template, as every theme has different ways of installation process.

After you install your template, you need to see what preferences are needed for exact theme.

In most of the times, you need to change image sizes and performance. Do not forget to rearrange icons.

Congratulation! Your theme is installed and set up correctly. Time to correct selling features of your store.

5

SHIPPING, TAXES AND LOCALIZATION

Localization.

Your store can be created in any language, for any country and with any currency. To add a language to your store you can open Localization menu and choose a language you need.

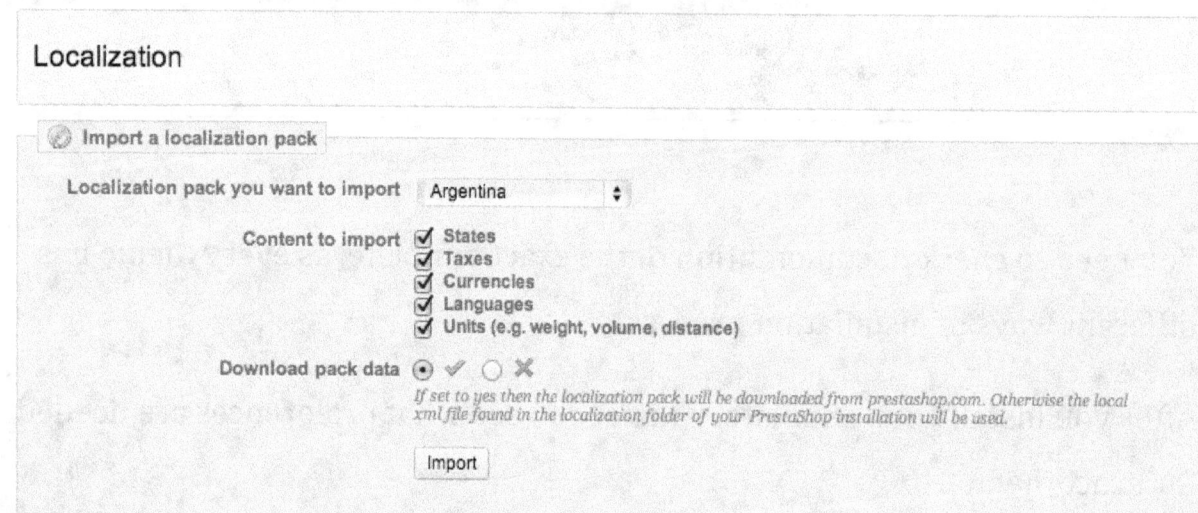

Select content you want to import and press "Import". The language will be automatically installed in your prestashop store. If you want to disable or enable any language you need to open Language menu, click on a language and change a status or click on a green checkmark ✓.

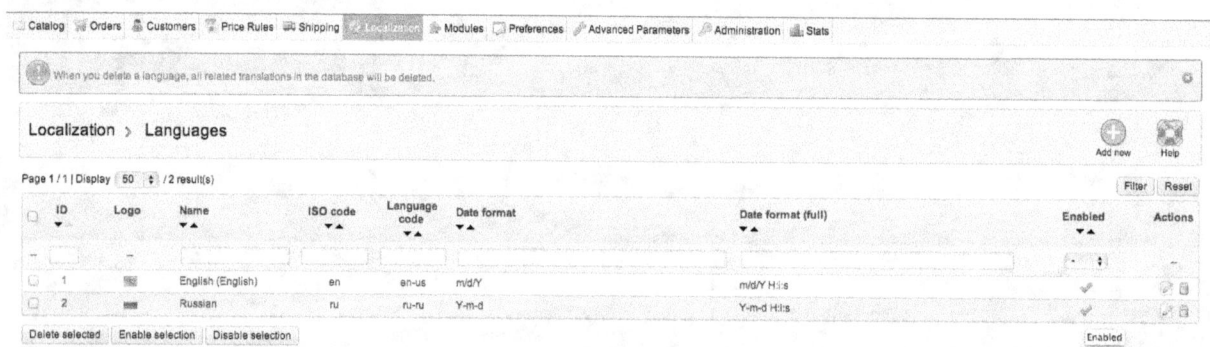

The same way you can also add and edit Zones, Countries, States, Currencies, and Taxes.

Taxes.

Your Prestashop store comes already preprogrammed with Tax rates and you do not have to do any changes to it, but if you need to add a new tax rate, you can do it with the following steps.

To add or change a tax rate you need to open "Localization"-> "Taxes"

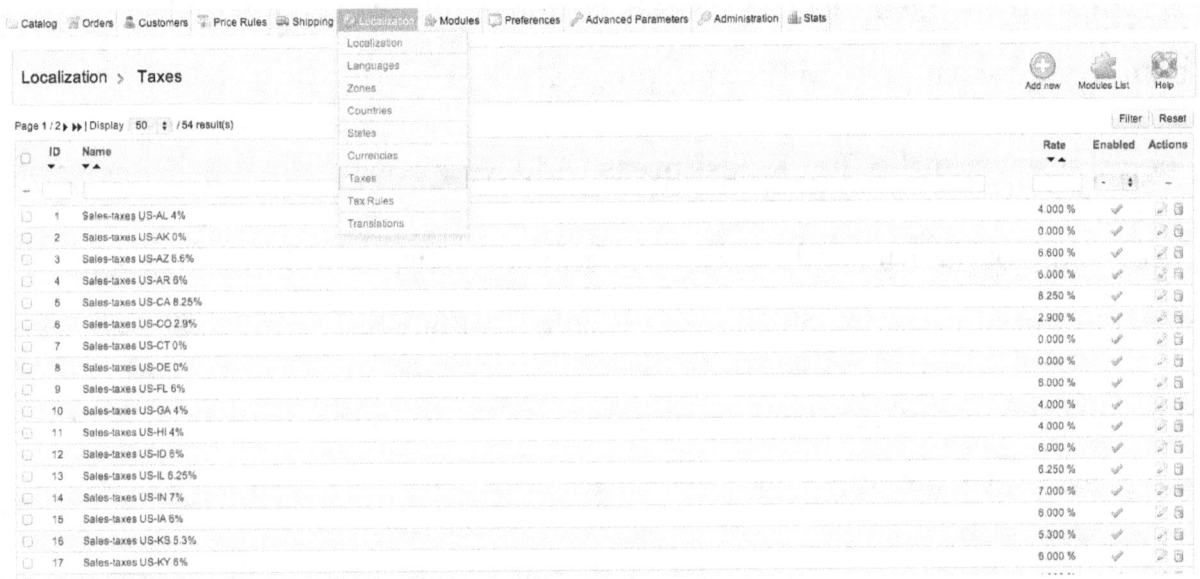

Press "Add New" or select one you want to change. If you are adding a new Tax rate you need to enter a name and percentage % of tax rate you want to add.

Press "Save".

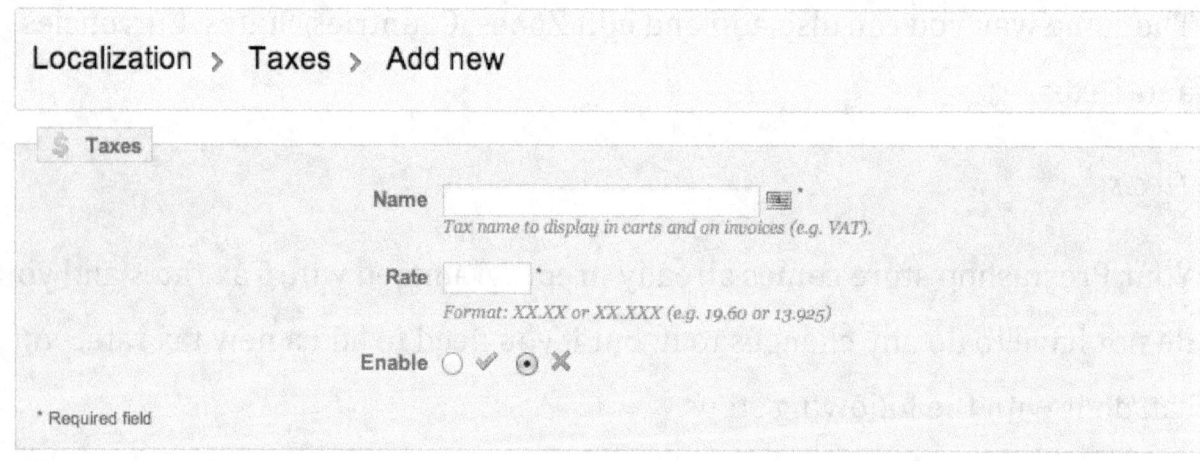

You can also enable or disable taxes here and allow or disallow to display them to your customers in the shopping cart.

Open "Localization"->"Tax Rules" press "Add New".

Enter name of the rule and press "Save and Stay". Press Add New Tax Rule Select Country zip code behavior of tax rule if applicable.

Select a Tax Rate, which you have created earlier from the drop down menu and press "Save and Stay".

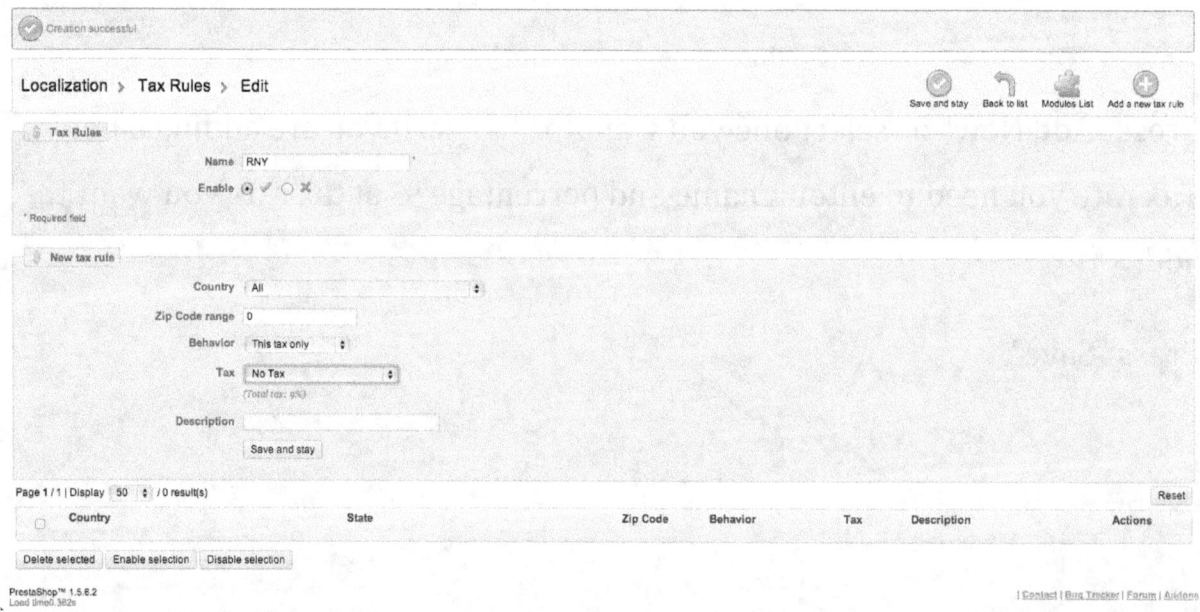

Your tax rules are ready and will be added to shopping cart of your customers when they shop at your store.

If you need to change any default name in your store, for example, from "Manufacturers" to "Partners" or anything what can't be changed or translated automatically, you can open "Translation", select a theme and press on a flag next to it. Find the name which you wish to change and type new name next to it.

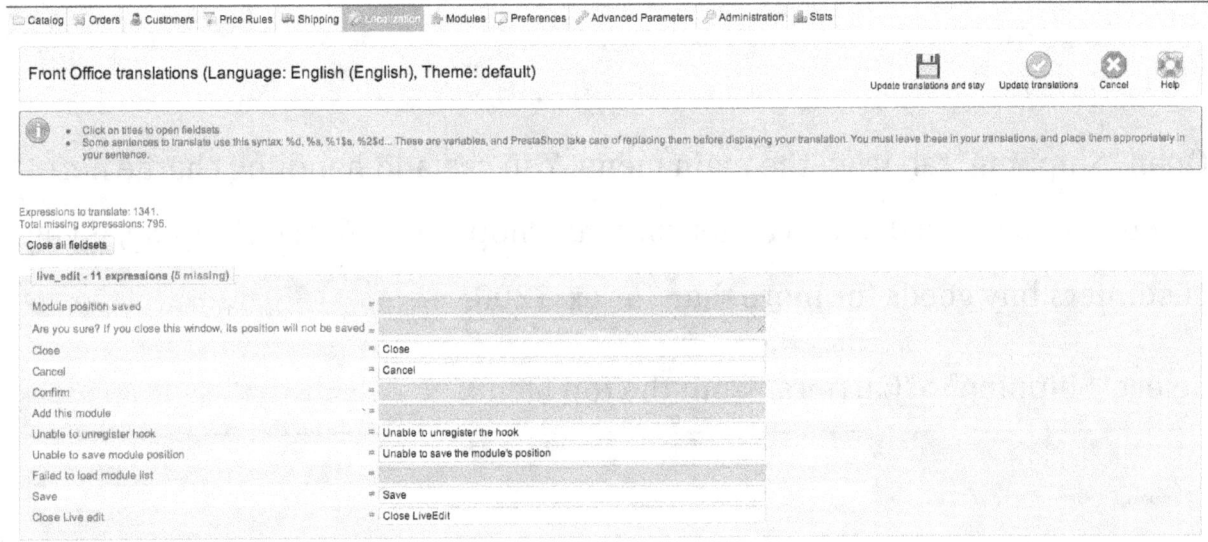

Press "Save".

Shipping.

You can use different types of shipping options in your store.

You can use custom carriers and rates.

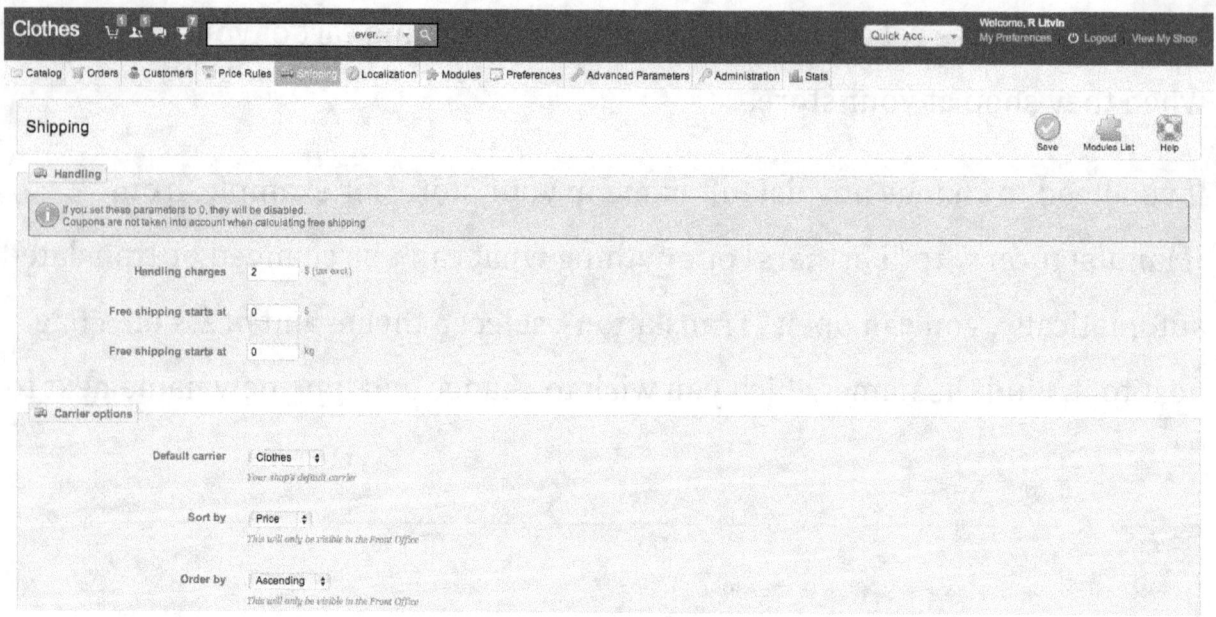

Open "Shipping" tab from the main menu. You can add handling charge here, as well as Change a default carrier for your shop and add free shipping, if your customers buy goods for more than for ex. $200.

Select "Shipping"->"Carriers" from the top Menu.

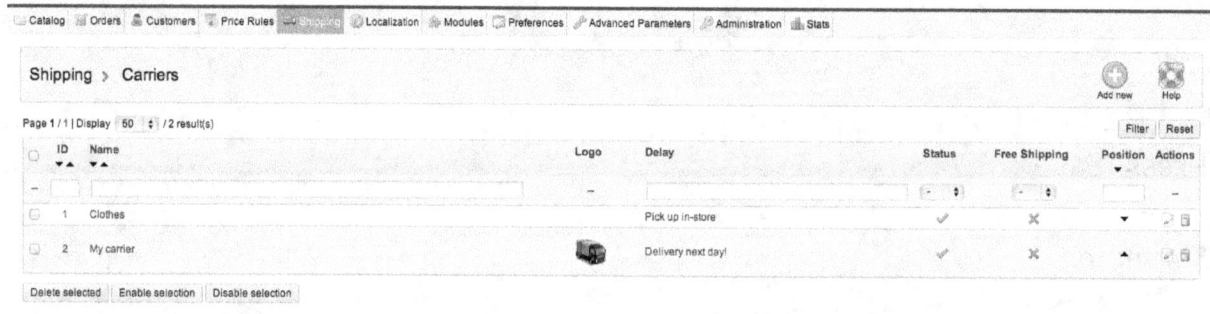

Press "Add New" and enter a Carrier name, for example: USPS

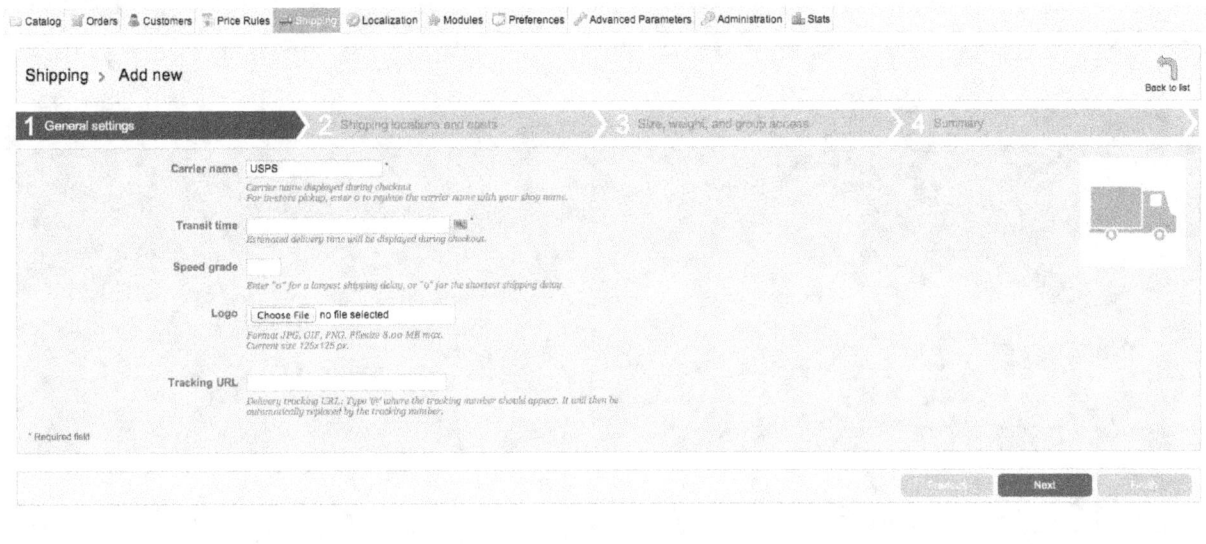

Enter speed grade and transit time and select a carrier logo picture from your computer. Press "Next". Select ✓ if Handling rate is included in the price of shipping.

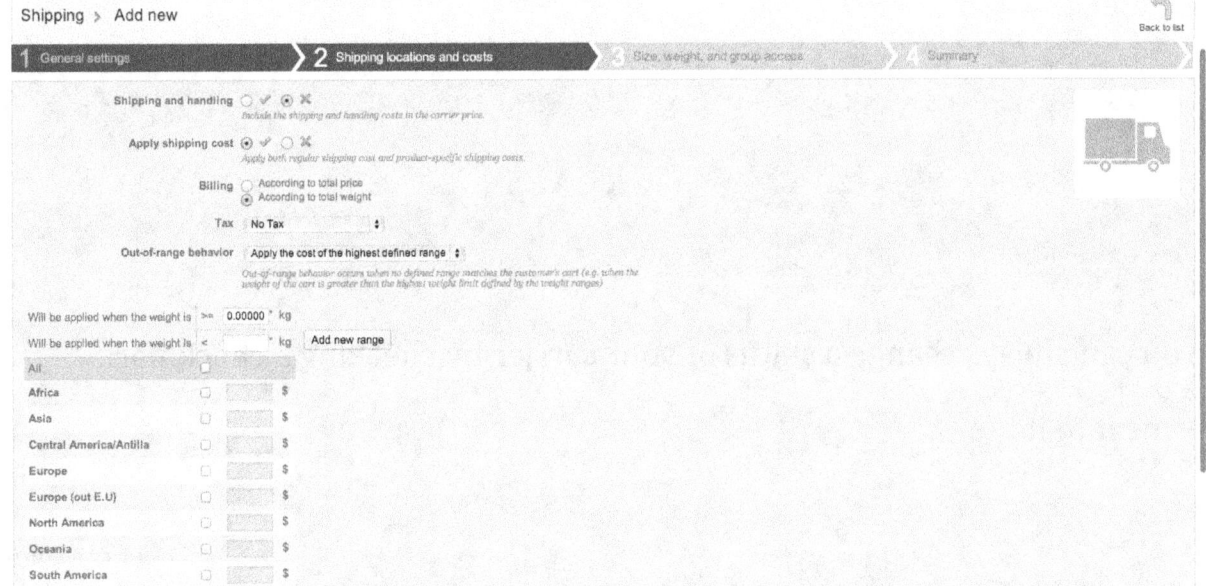

Select ✓ if you want to add Tax to your shipping cost. Indicate weight for which you want to add additional shipping cost. Enter amount you want to charge for Shipping and press "Next".

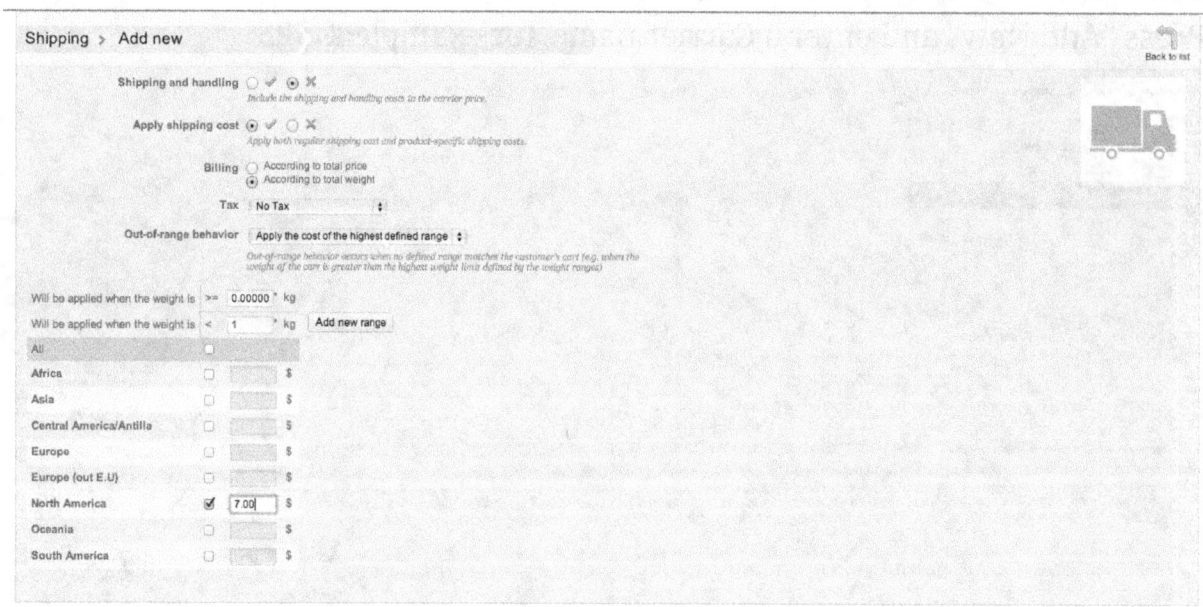

You can also enter Maximum package size and weight. Press "Finish". Your shipping carrier was created and is ready to use.

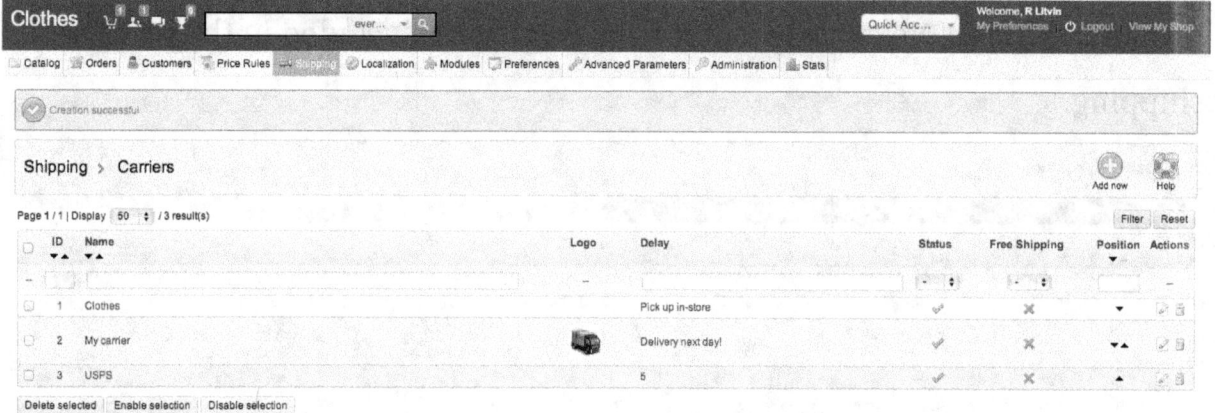

You can always change a status of your carrier by checking a checkmark ✓ next to it.

6
PAYMENTS PROCESSING

There are unlimited types of payment solutions for your store but I will talk about 3 most common ones: Wire transfer & Checks, PayPal and Credit Cards.

To get paid by wire transfer or by check, the first thing you need is a Bank Account. After that, in order to get paid, you need to provide your account details to your customers.

Open "Modules"->"Payments". Locate "Payment by Check" module and press "Configure". Specify name and address required for the customer to send payment. Press "Update Settings".

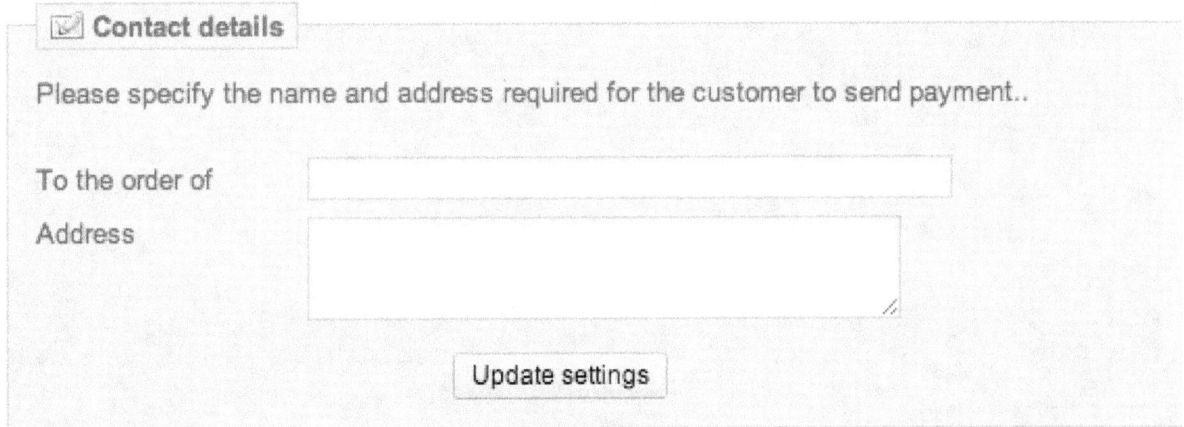

Your Checks Payment solution is ready!

Open "Modules"->"Payments" and locate "Bank Wire" module. Press "Configure" and enter bank details, name and address. Press "Update" settings and your bank wire transfer payment solution is up and running!

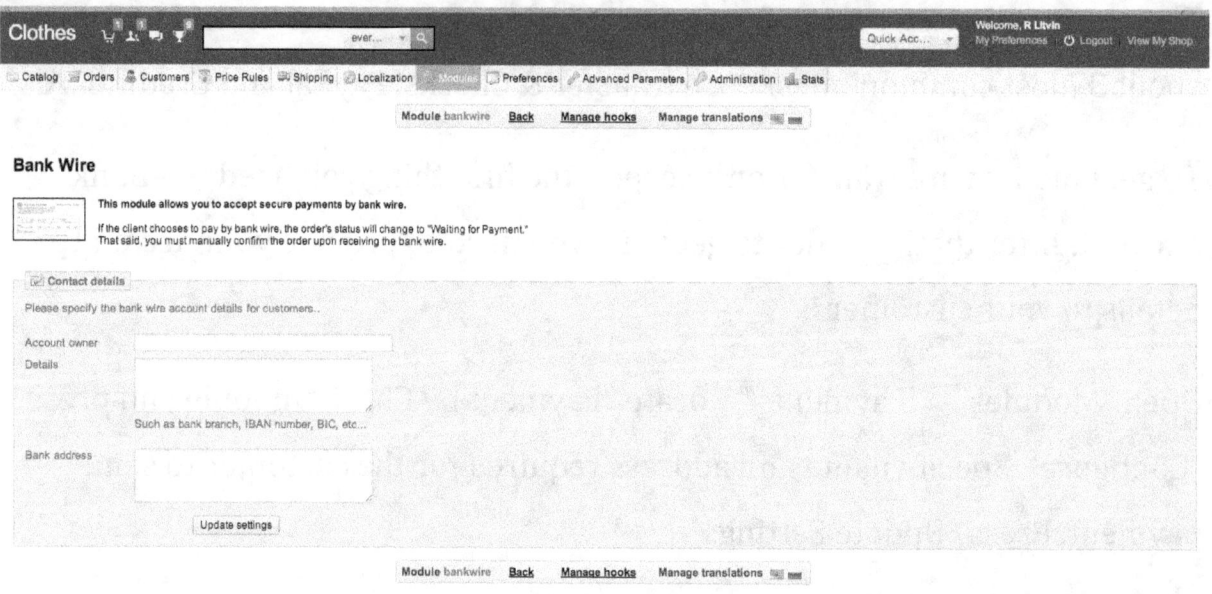

Open "Modules"-> Locate "PayPal Module" and press "install".

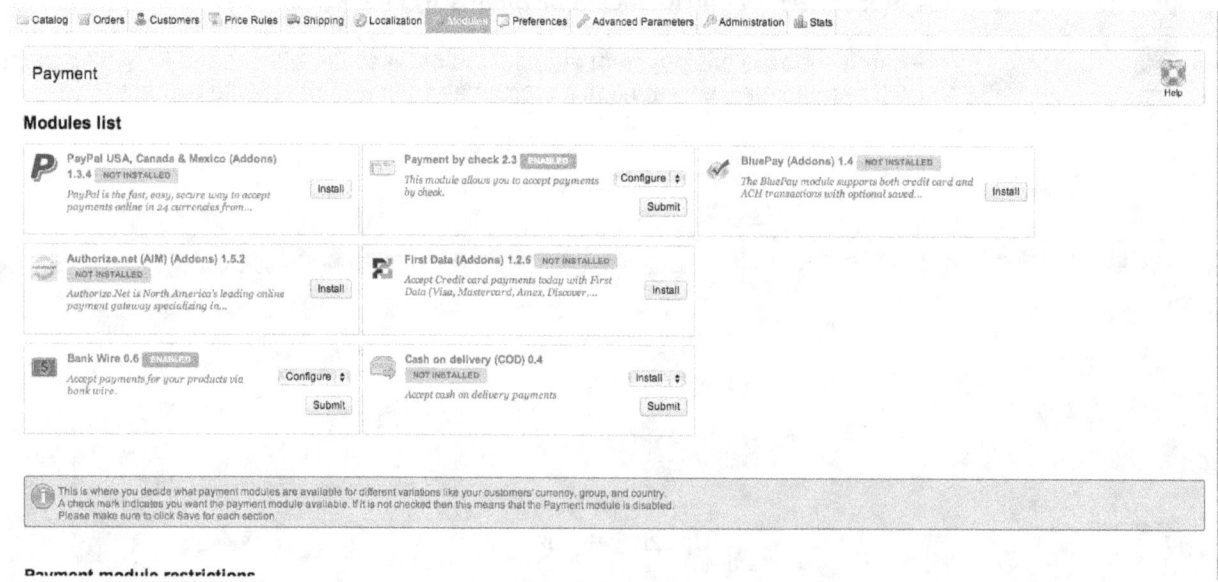

In the window that opens, you can choose few different options to accept payments.

We use PayPal Express Checkout system. Just put a mark next to Paypal Express Checkout and press "Enable PayPal Express Checkout Only"

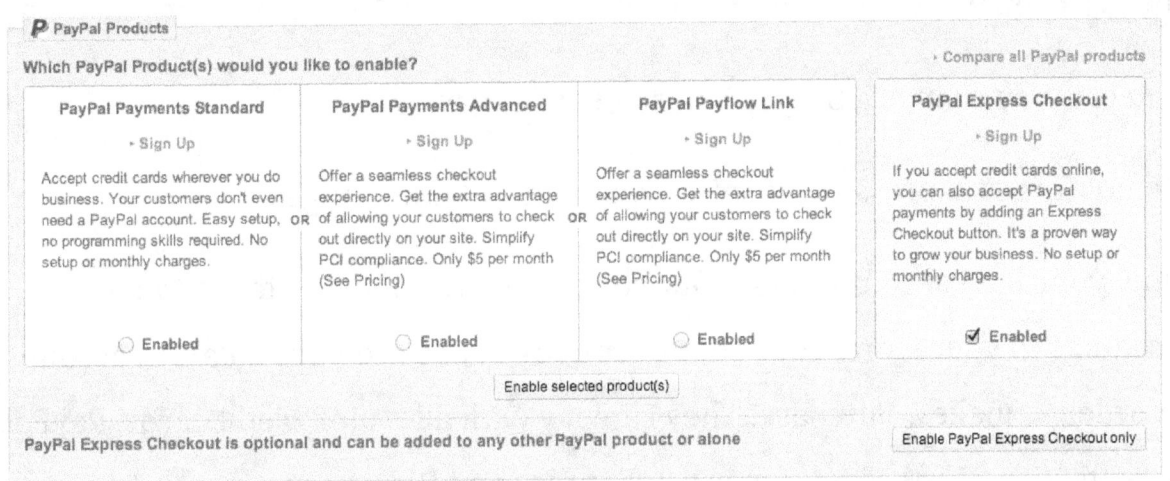

Scroll down and fill out PayPal Business account, API Username, API password and API signature.

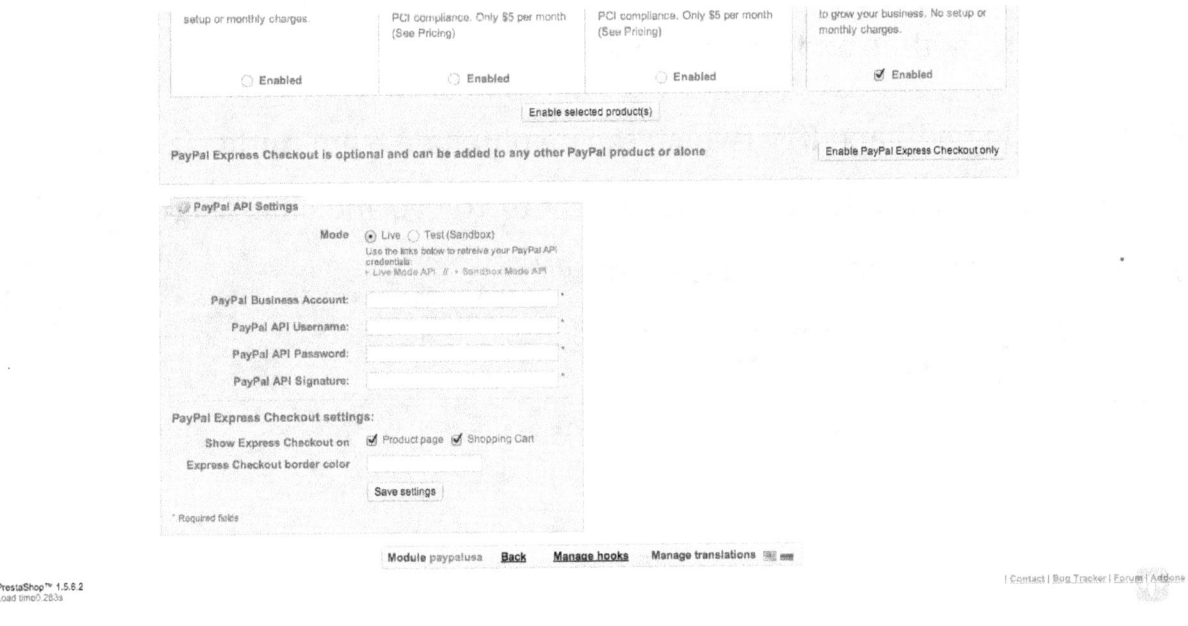

All this info can be obtained from your PayPal account. You can contact PayPal, if you can't find this information on your account.

You can also put your PayPal payment in a test mode, so there will be no actual transactions going through the terminal, and you can test as many times as you wish.

You can also change a border color of PayPal box.

Do not forget to press "Save" after you made all the changes.

Now your PayPal solution for your store is ready. You can start adding products to your store. Your customer doesn't need to have a PayPal account in order to make a purchase. They can pay with all major credit cards. PayPal accepts Visa, Mastercard, American Express and Discovery.

If you wish to use your own merchant, you can process your transactions through Authorize.net add-on. Just open "Modules" ->"Payments", locate Authorize.net add-on and press "INSTALL".

Enter your login ID and Key (which can be obtained from Authorize.net account). Choose production environment to go live and choose credit cards you wish to accept. Press "Update Settings".

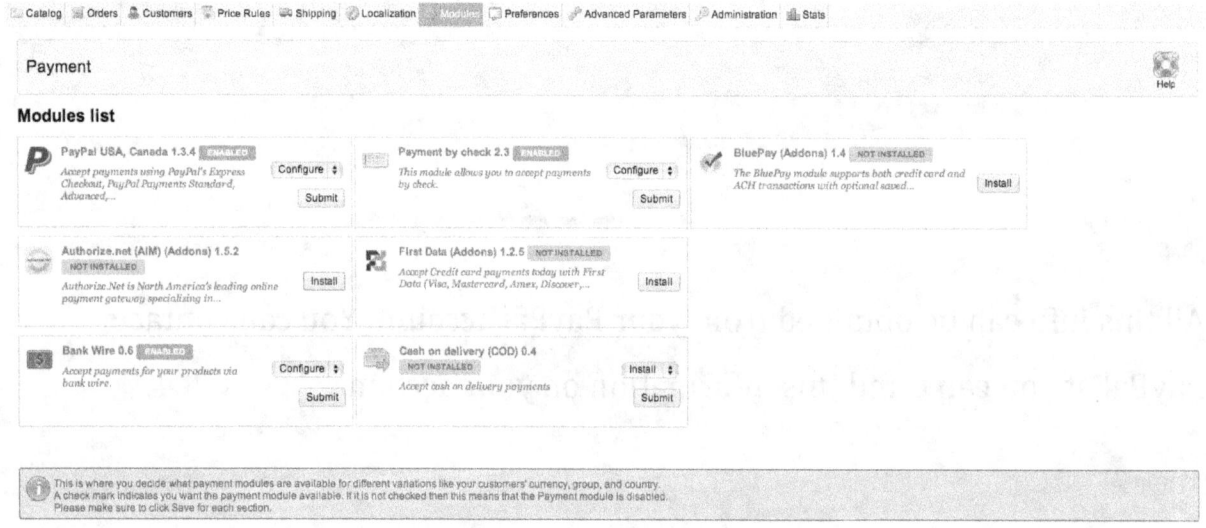

All your payment solutions have been setup correctly.

You can always ask for assistance from your payment merchant, if you are not sure about your login credentials.

Please note that your API login credentials are different from your account login.

7
ADDING PRODUCTS AND CATEGORIES

In this chapter I want to show you all options of adding products from your existing database or creating a new product.

Let's start from creating a new Category.

Open "Catalog"-> "Categories" and press "Add New".

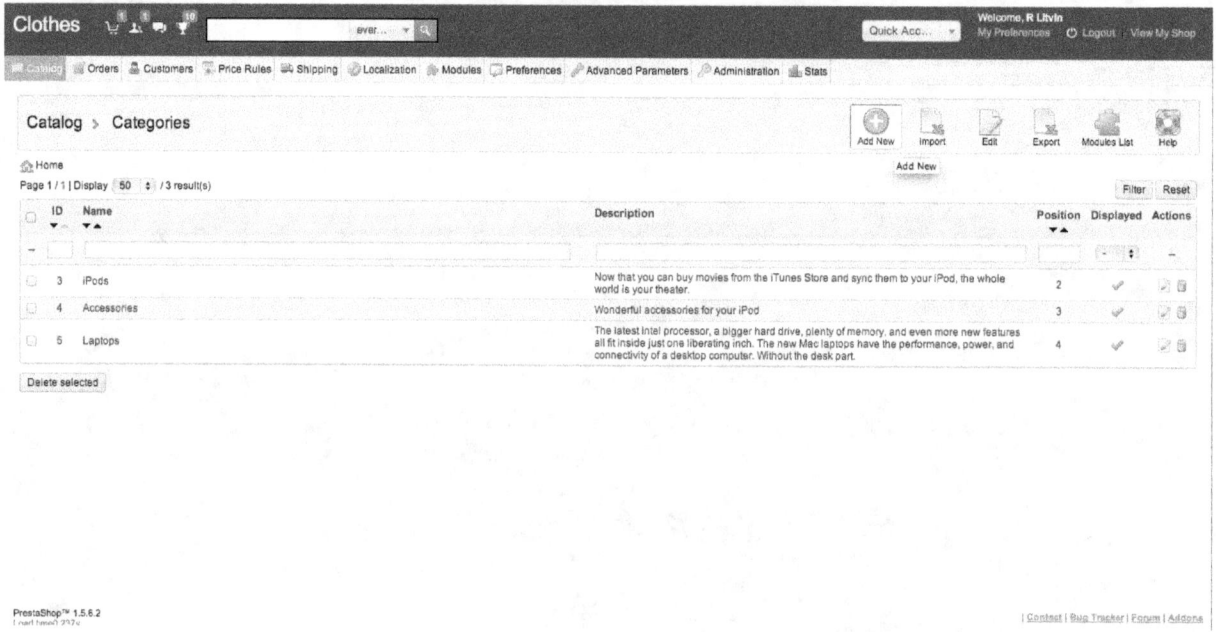

Enter name of the category and parent category.

Parent category can be any main category. For example, if you sell cosmetics you can have categories: "soaps" and "oils". In the "soap" category you can have subcategories like, "aromatic soap", "body soaps" and "facial soaps".

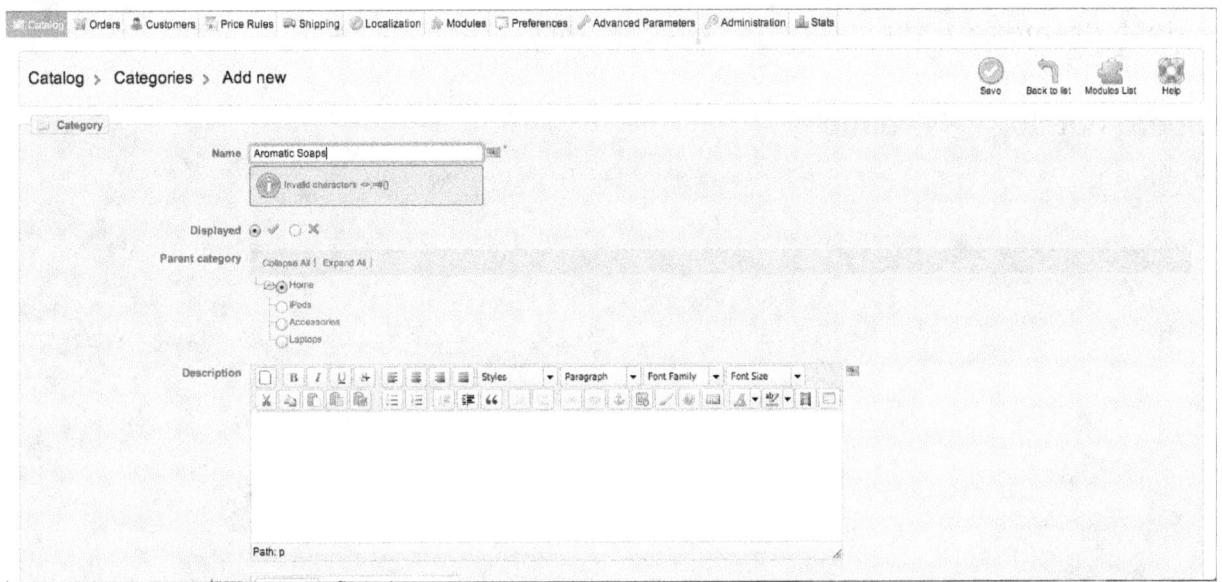

Enter description of your category and choose an icon for this category from your computer.

Press "Save".

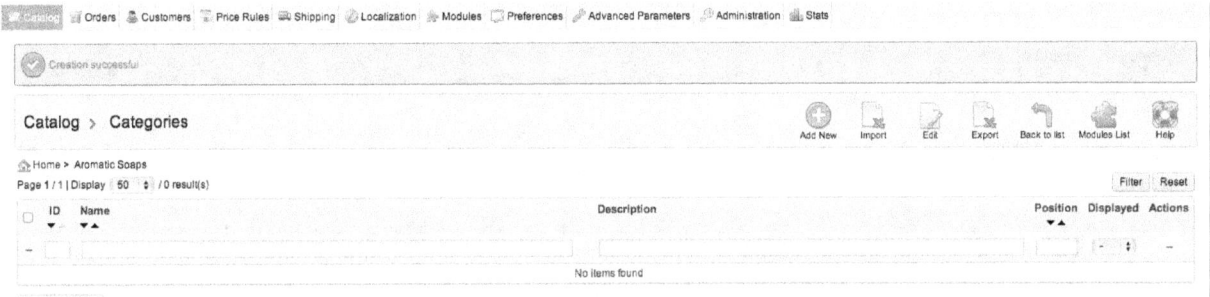

Now your category is ready and you can open home tab to see it.

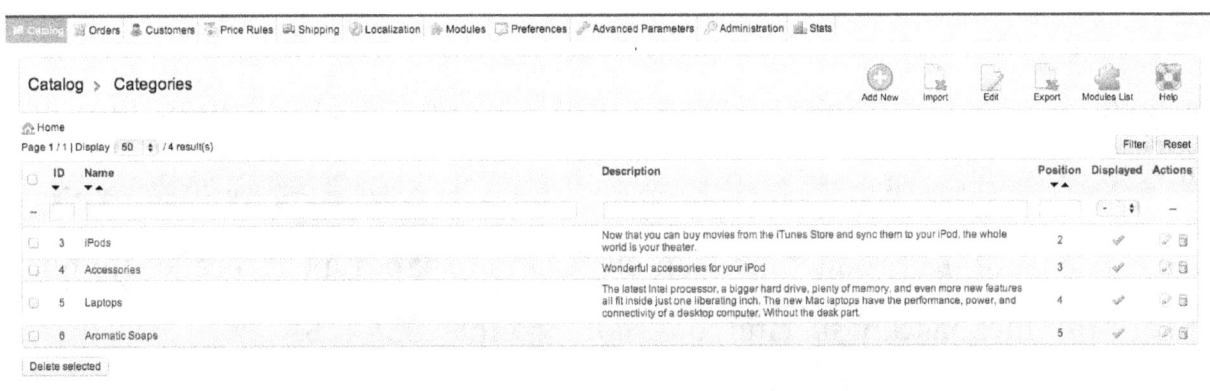

43

Now it's time to add product to this category.

Open "Catalog"->"Products".

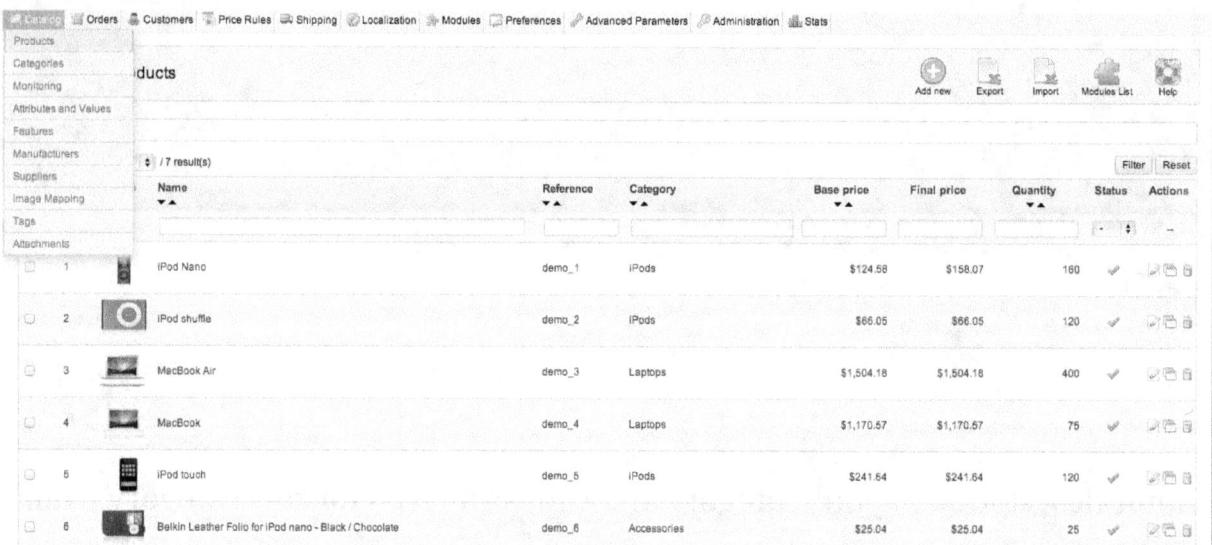

You will see a list of sample products there, which you can delete. Press "Add New" product.

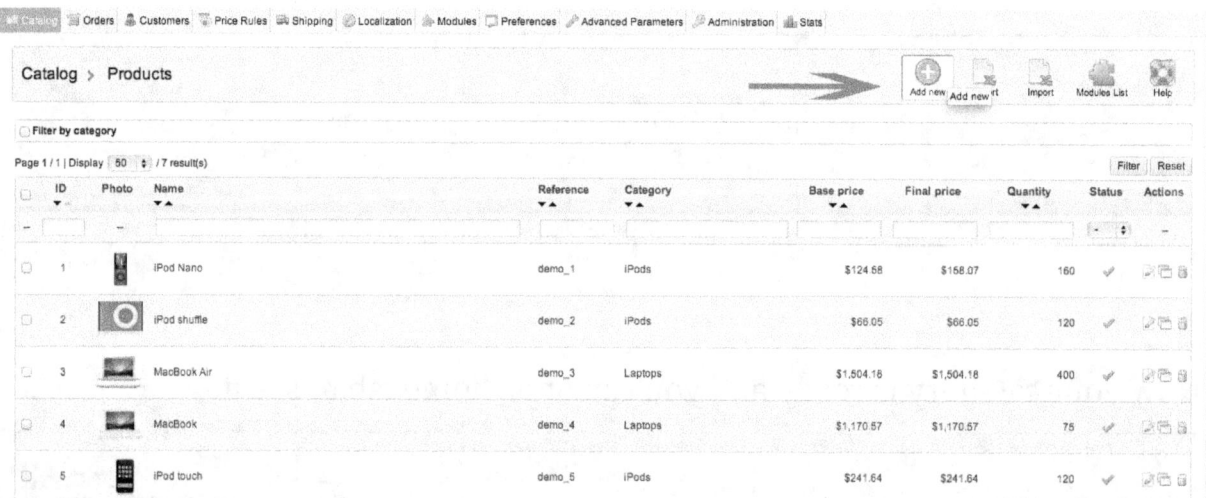

You will see a screen where you can add or edit product information for every of your products.

Type a name of the product for example "Lemon Soap" type reference number if your product has any specific code. For example: 554435.

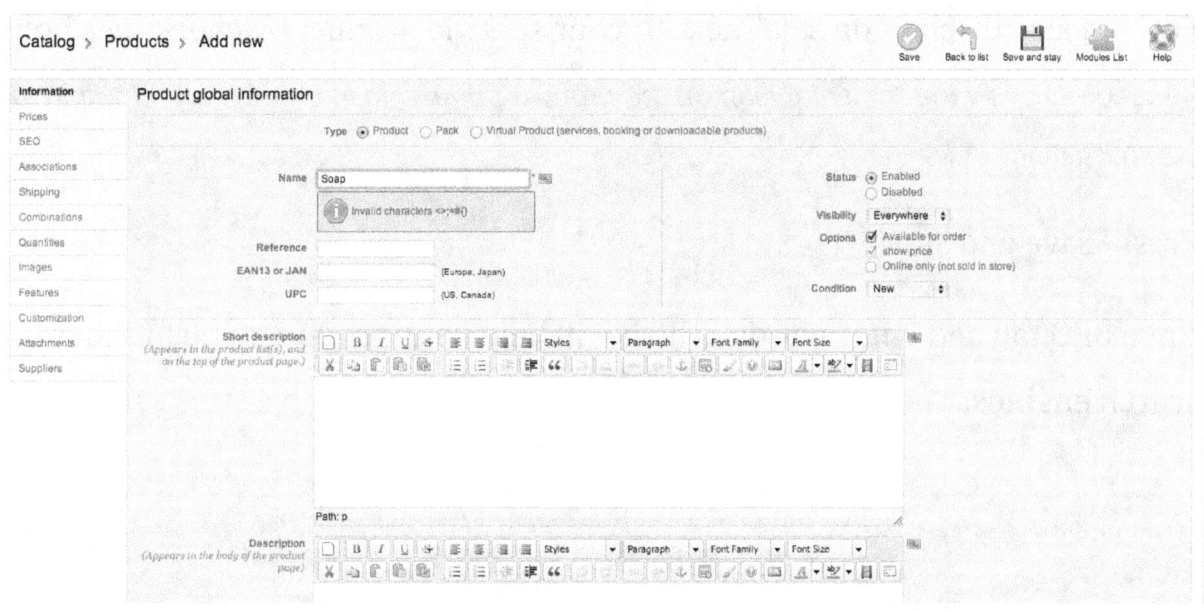

Enter short description of your product, for example: Delicate soap bar for oily skin. Enter full description in the field below, for example: Delicate soap bar for oily skin. It can be used every day to make you look beautiful and young. You can also add tags for your product, allow ordering of this product or show the condition of your product on this page. After that, press "Save and Stay". Press on the tab "Prices" and enter product cost, for example $5, and product price that you wish your product to be sold for, for example $10. Choose tax rule for your state.

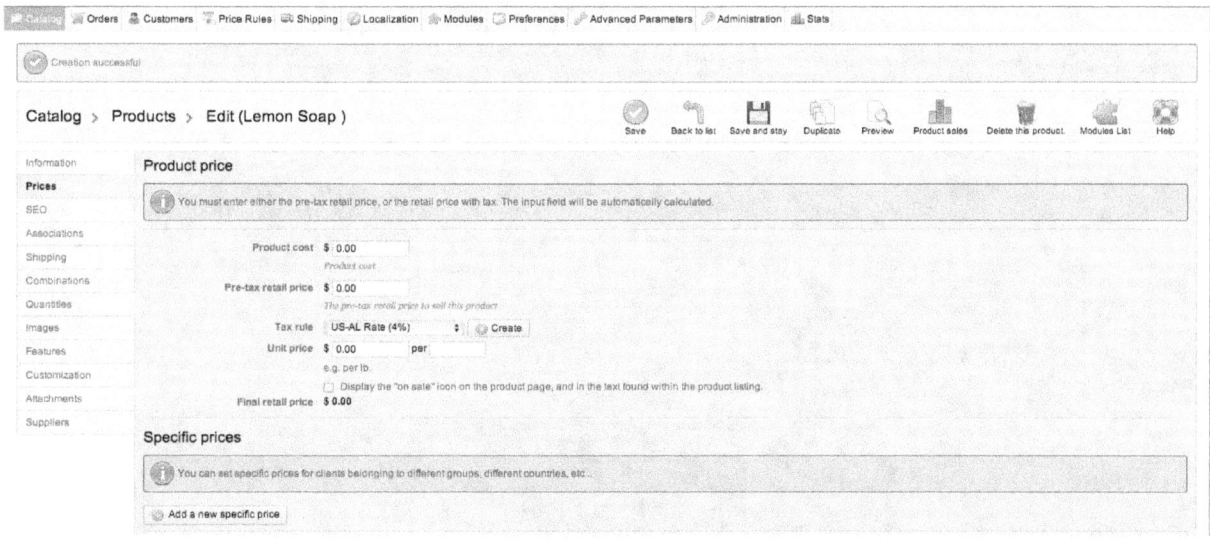

You can also display "on sale" next to your specific product by checking a box next to - *Display the "on sale" icon on the product page, and in the text found within the product listing.*

Press "Save and Stay".

Open SEO tab and enter words, which will help your product to be found on search engines.

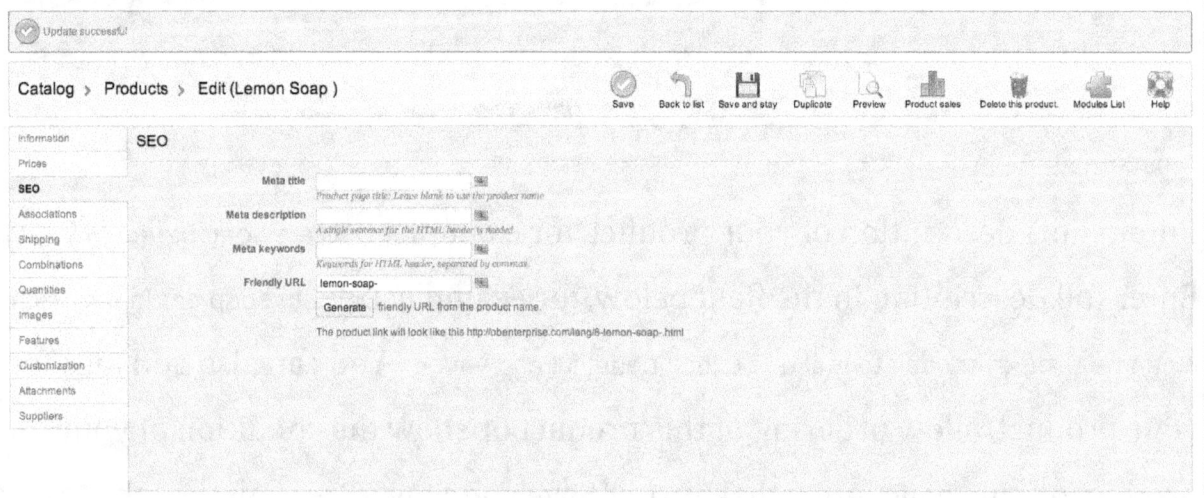

Press "Save and Stay".

Open "Associations" tab to add your product to specific categories.

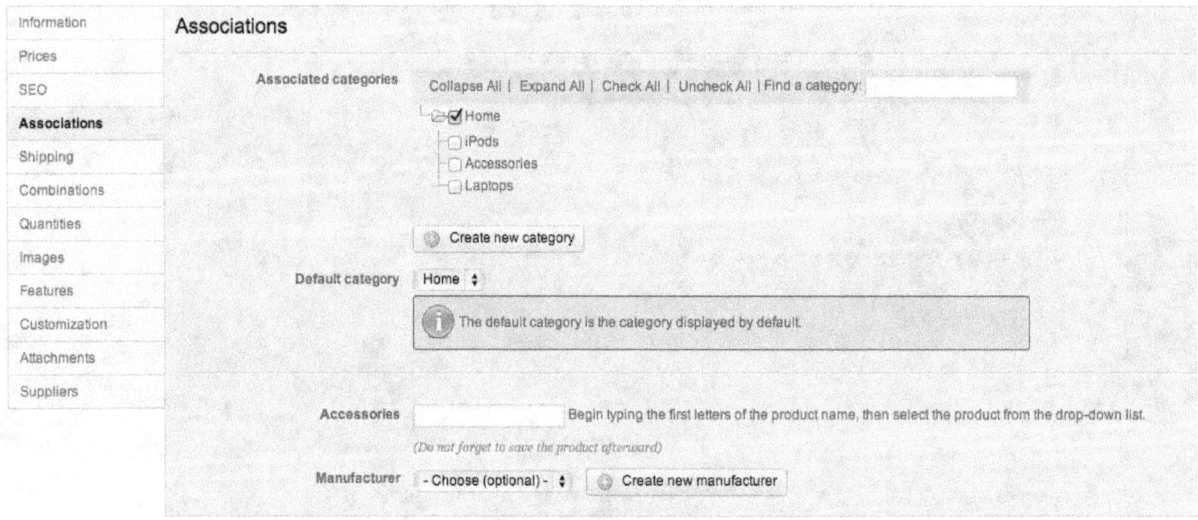

Please note that all products that are in Home category will be automatically displayed in your featured product box. Press "Save and Stay". Open "Shipping" Tab, if you wish to add package sizes or choose specific shipping carriers for this product, or you can leave it by default.

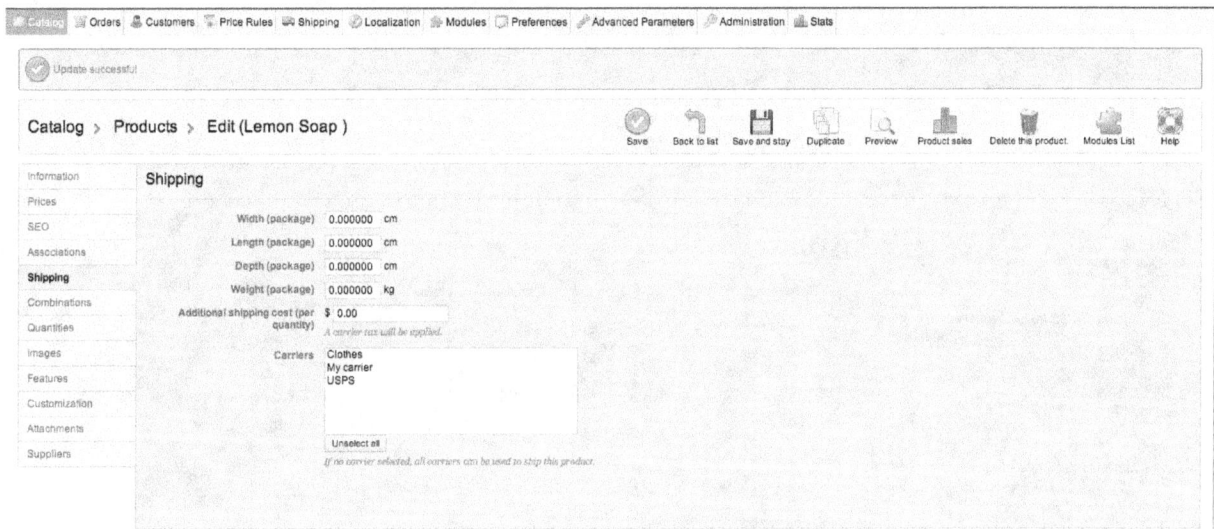

Open "Combinations" tab and press "Generate"

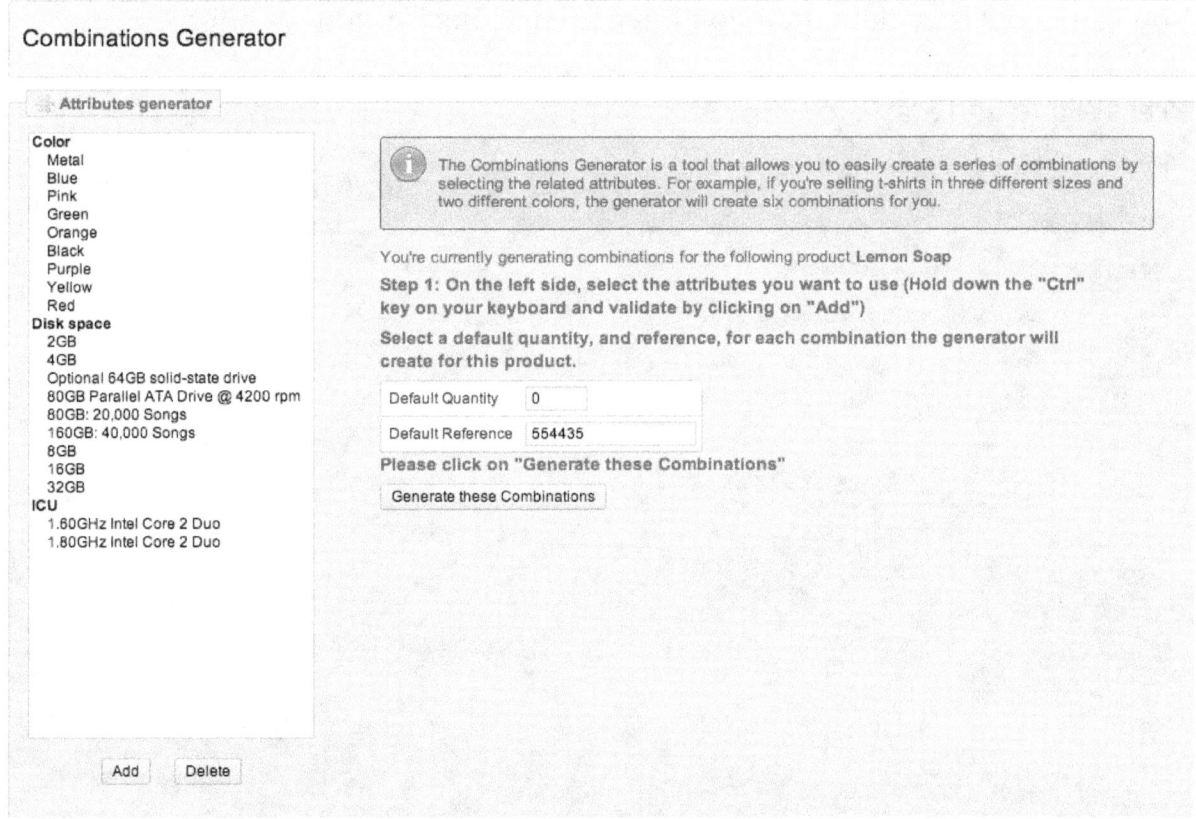

Here you can add product options and features, so your customer can choose different product options.

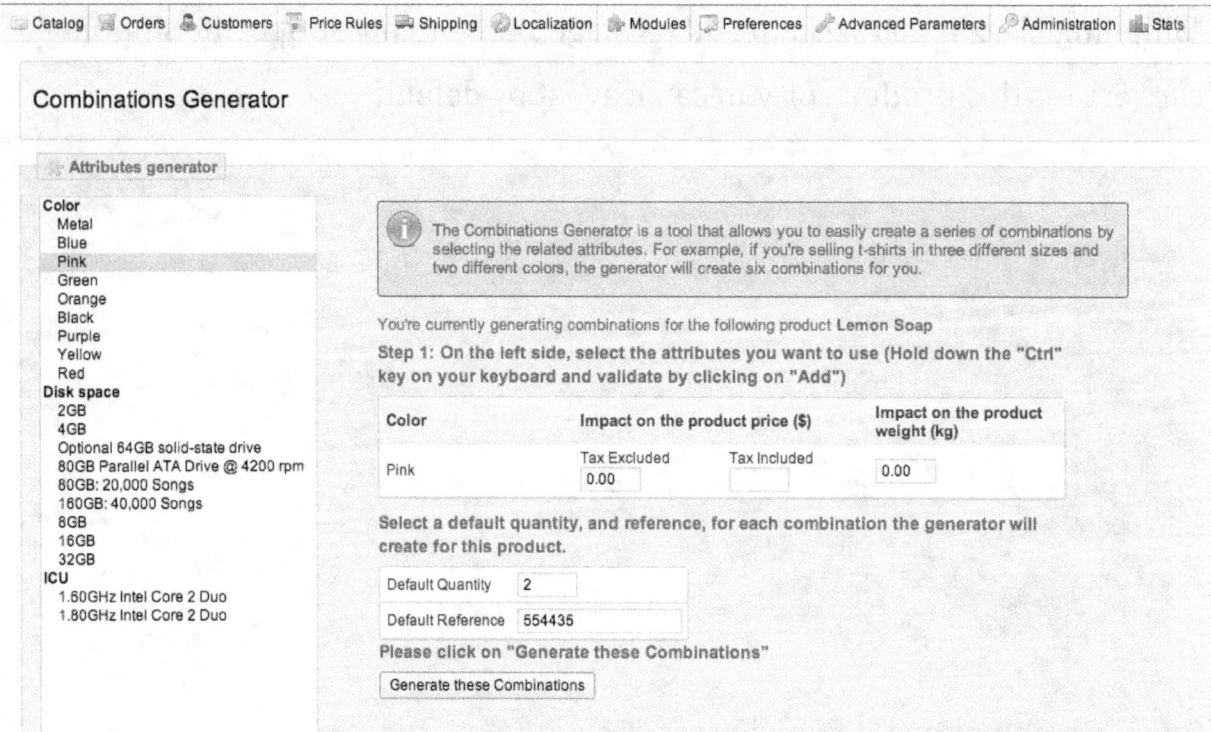

You can leave it by default, if you have no options for your product.

Press "Save and Stay".

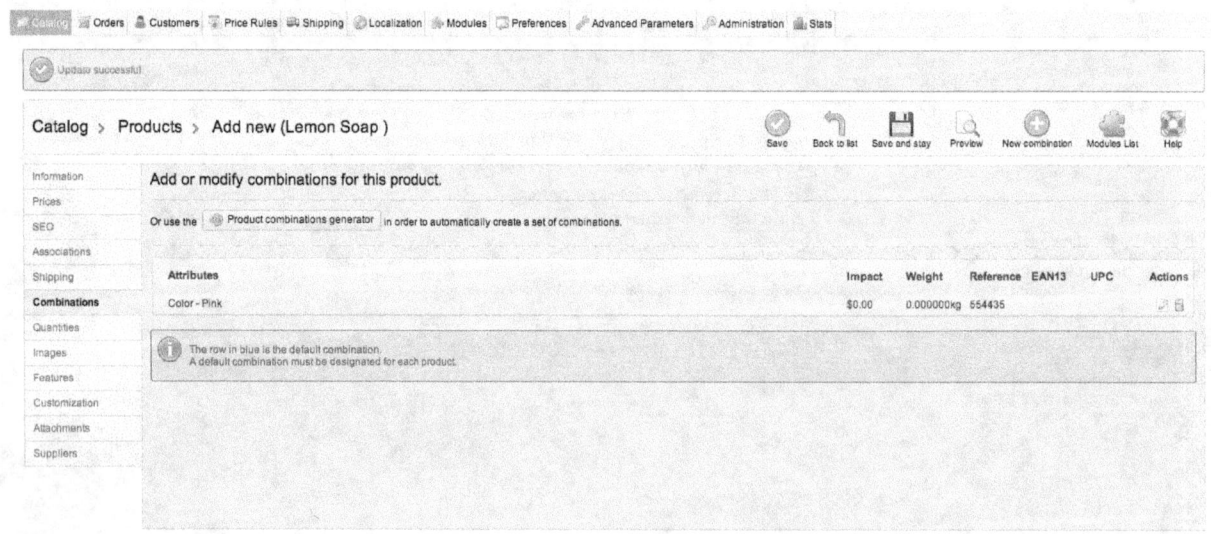

Open "Quantity" tab to enter quantity of products you have on hand, ready to ship to your customers.

Press "Save and Stay".

Open "Images" Tab and upload an image of this product from your computer.

Press "Save and Stay".

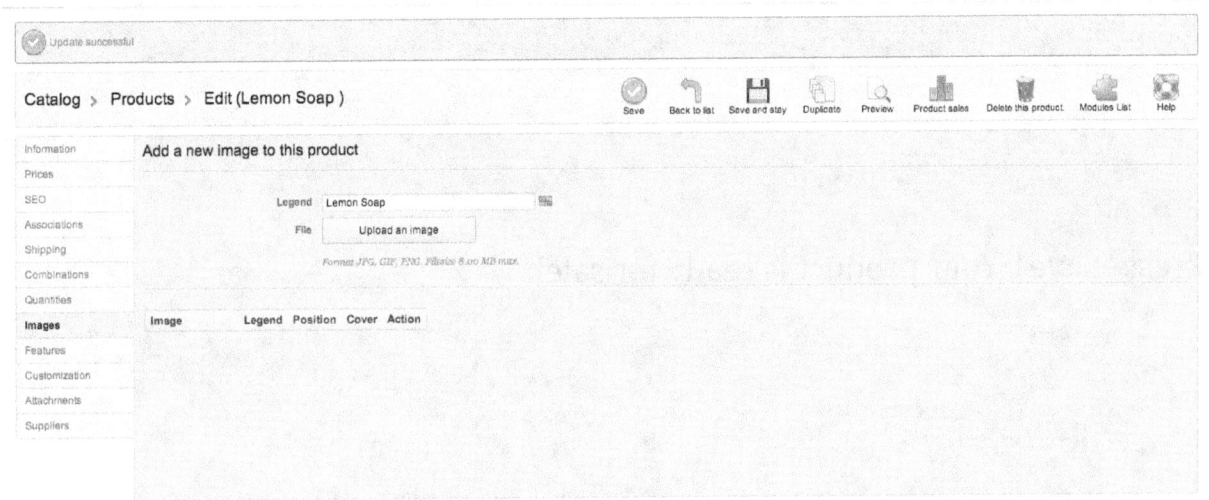

You can also add features for this product, customize fields, choose suppliers or upload a virtual product, if it's a song or ebook, or if you want to include a user manual for your product.

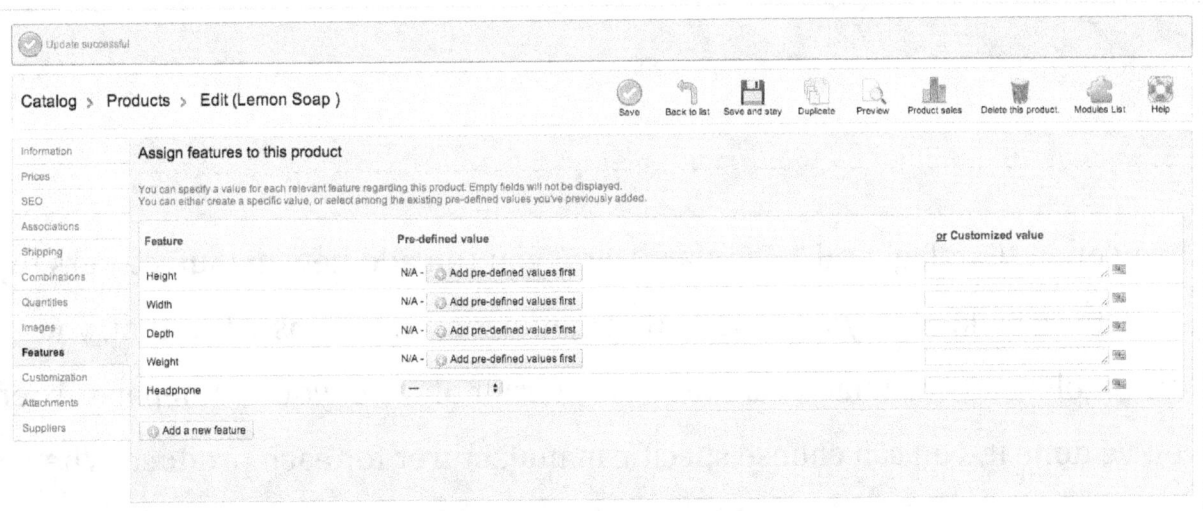

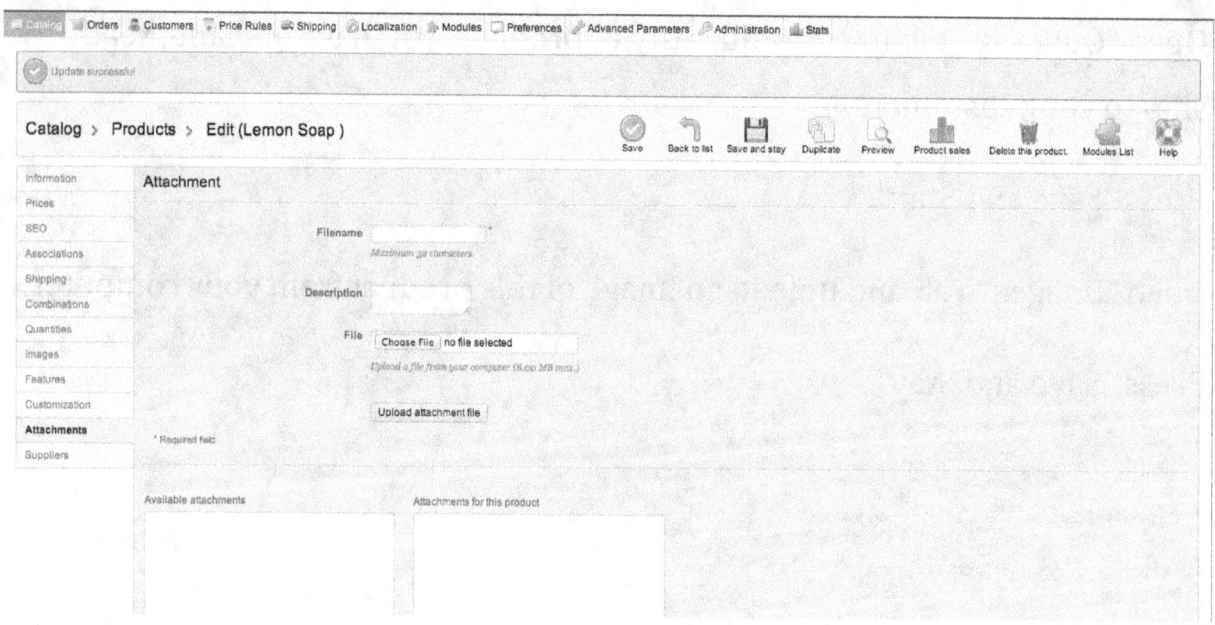

Press "Save". Your product is ready for sale!

If you open "Catalog" and "Manufacturers" you can add new manufacturers to your store. Make sure you've uploaded manufacturers' logos. After that, you can enable your manufacturers to show in front office of your homepage. After you've done it, you can choose specific manufacturer for each product. When your customers press on specific manufacturer, all products will be displayed.

Prestashop automatically adjust each product for specific manufacturer that you choose and displays all that according to your customers' needs.

Moreover, all new products can be displayed on your homepage as well.

All products added to category "HOME" will be automatically added to your featured products. That way, if you install "Featured" module, you will be able to see all featured products on your homepage.

8
ORDERS PROCESSING

When your products are added to your store, payments and shipping are correctly setup, you can start processing orders.

Prestashop works on your orders automatically. It does not require any extra steps from you.

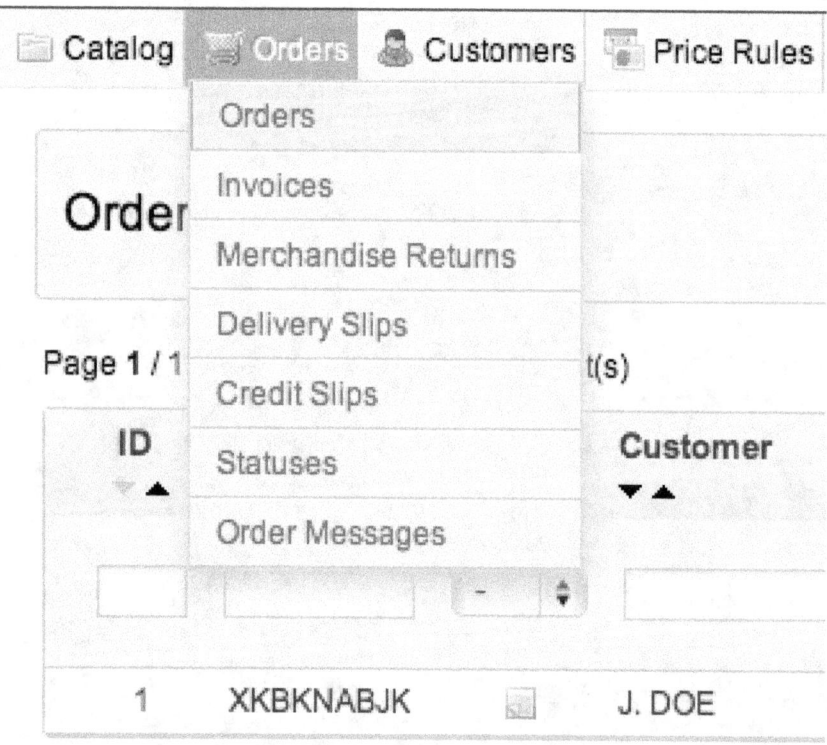

This is a professional engine that is perfect for every store.

After your customer placed an order in your store, you automatically receive an email with all necessary information: Customer's name, address and phone number, products he/she ordered and quantity, method and amount of payment. If you open "Orders" page, you can see a history of all orders ever placed on your website. You can click on any order and you will see full merchandizing solution for every business.

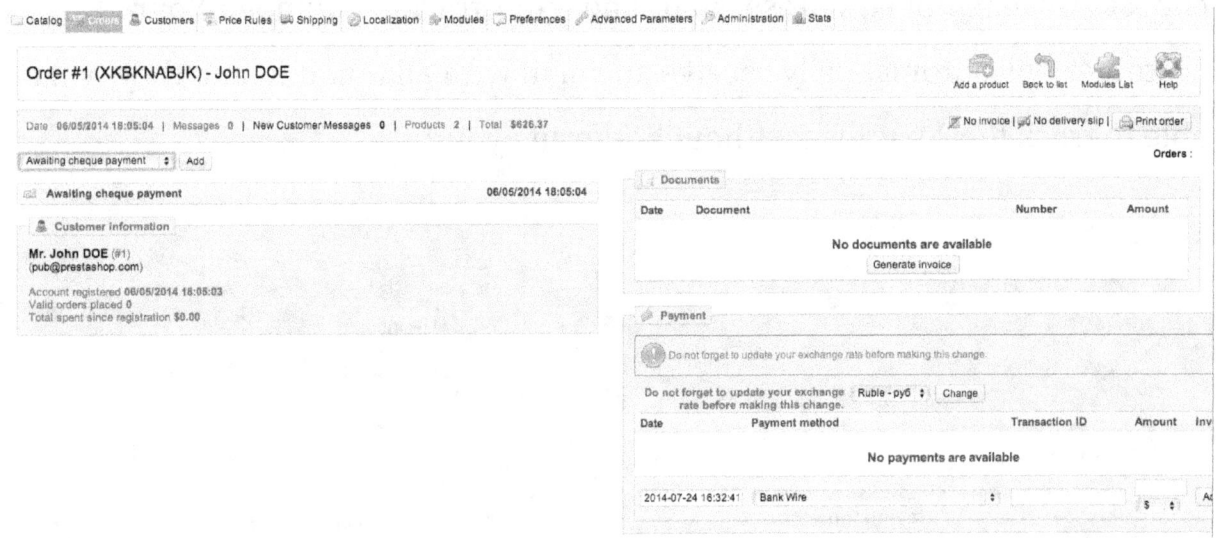

Customer can enter different shipping and billing addresses, as well as they can leave order comments about special delivery instruction or any other information.

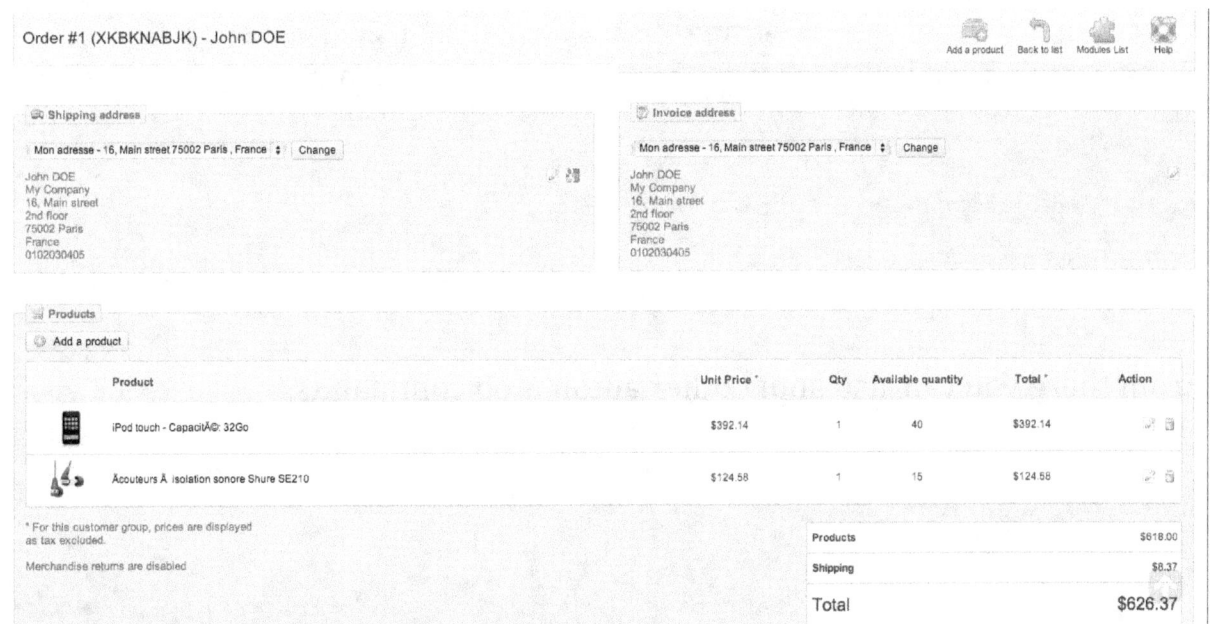

Also your Prestashop will automatically inform your customers via email about every step that is happening with their orders. For example, if you choose "Order shipped", press "Add" and enter tracking number. Your customer will automatically receive an email with all that info and they will be able to track their package without bothering you.

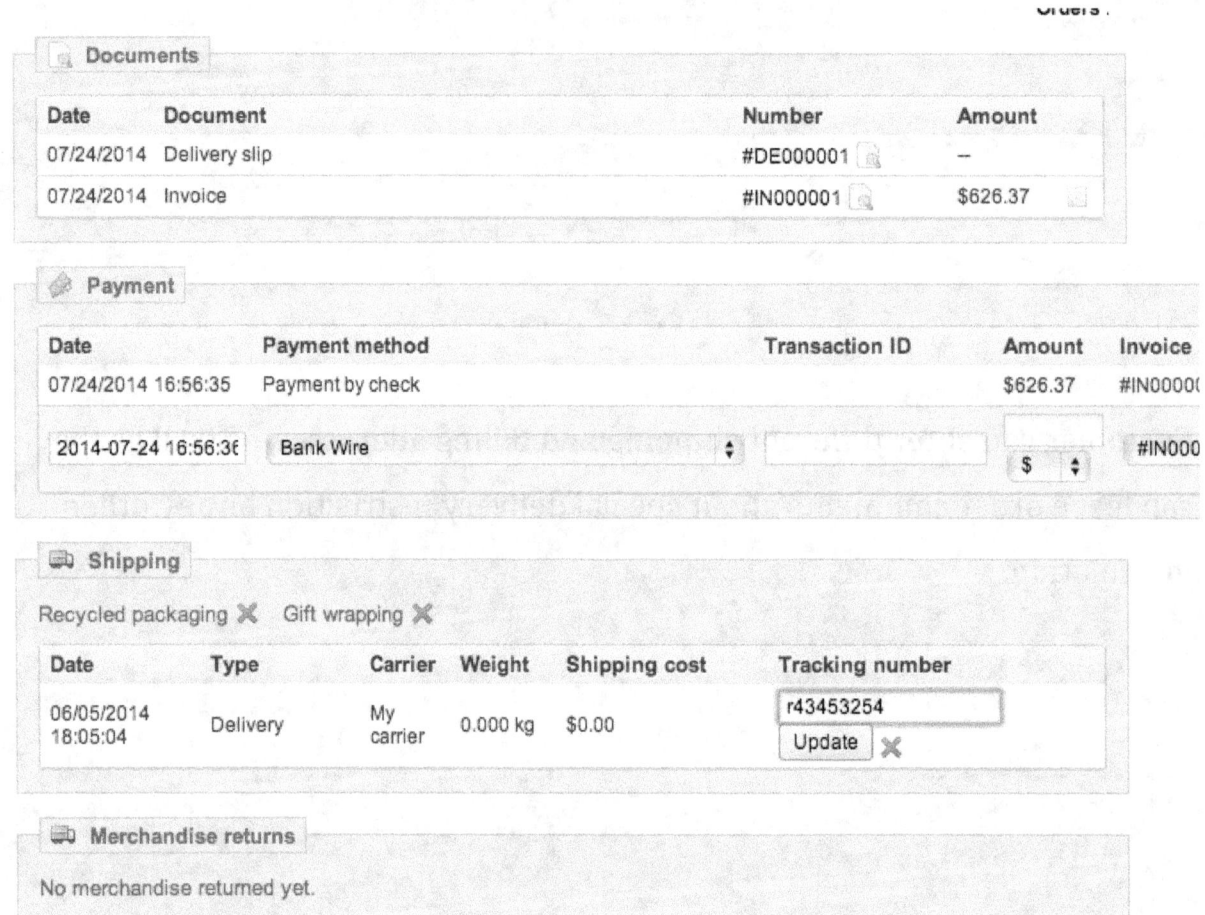

From there you can also apply other automated commands.

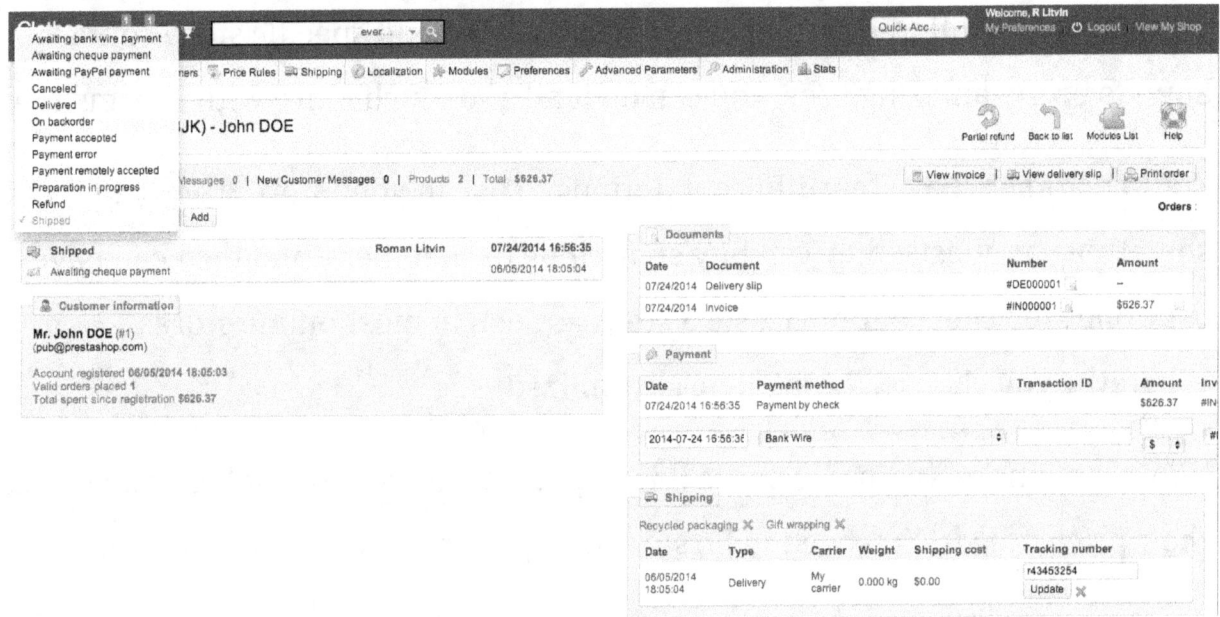

In "Orders" page you can also apply a specific discount to each order: just enter name, value of discount and press "Add".

You can generate PDF invoices, process merchandise returns and add your own order statuses. Plus you can add specific notes to be displayed for orders.

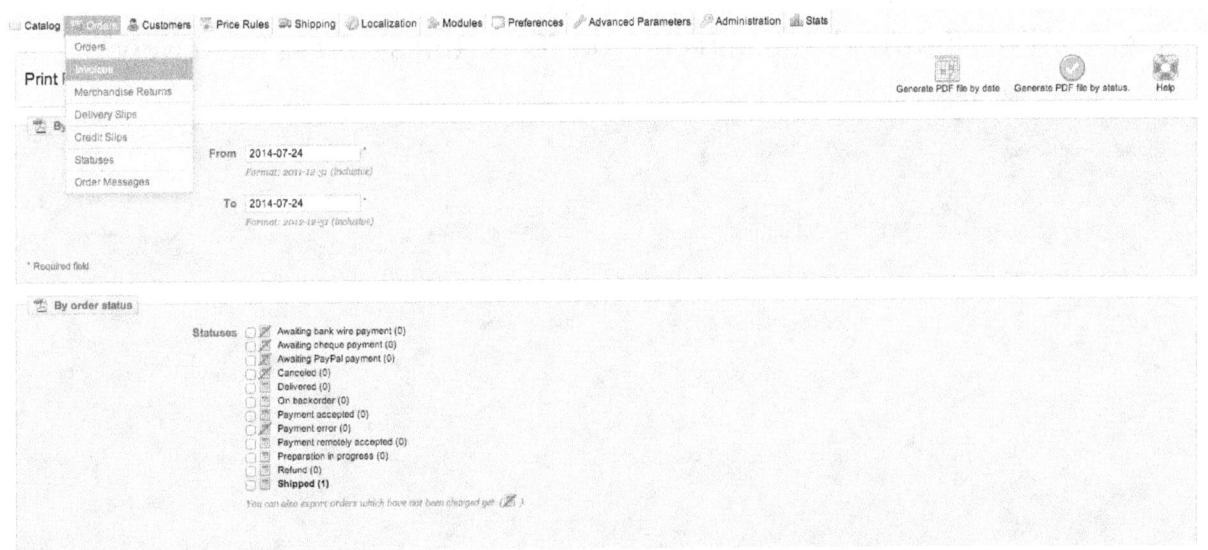

When you open "Customers" tab, you can find all needed information about every customer, who purchased something from your store, as well as customers, who created an account on your website.

You can create different groups for your store and add specific store contacts. Sounds pretty amazing? Yes, you can do it all and much more with Prestashop.

Your customers have few different options to use in your store. They can buy something as guests, they can buy something as members, and they can have easy one step checkout or classic 5 steps as seen in most online stores. Whatever you choose, it can all be customized.

When running an online business it is important to see other sellers and check their price ranges. You need to be sure, that your prices are not too high.

It is a big plus, if you run constant promotions and sales. You can create special discounts for specific products or for the whole store. For example, you can add code "SUMMER" to your store, and customers, who enter this code at the checkout, will get special discount, for example 20% for their entire purchase.

Just go to "PRICE RULES" tab and click on "Cart Rules". Press "Add New".

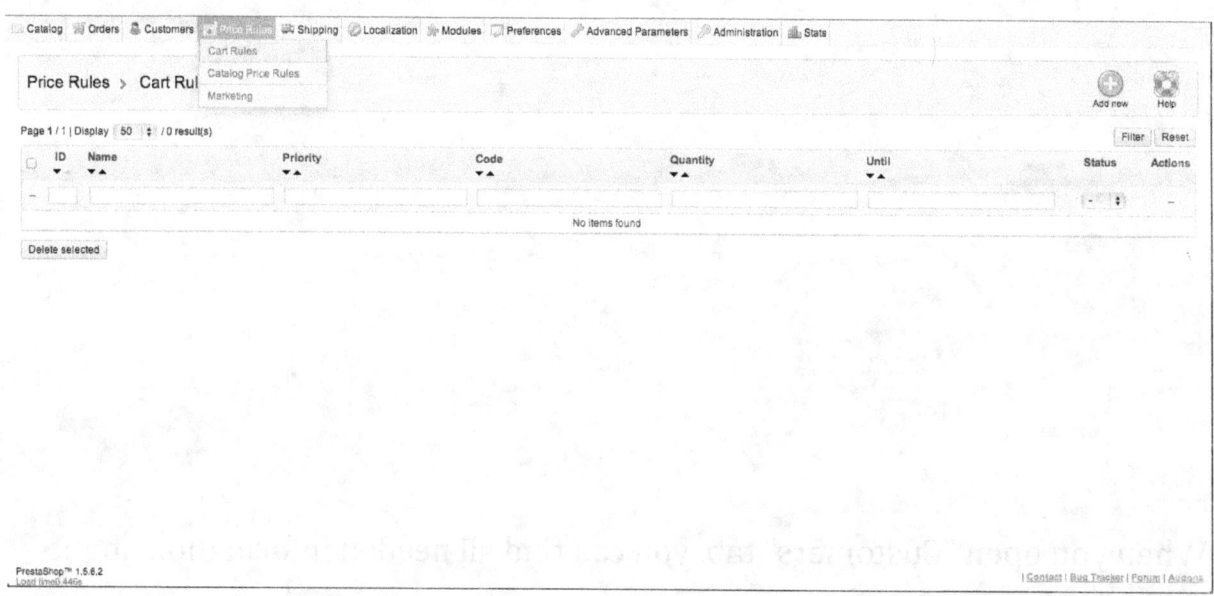

Enter the name of the promotion.

Enter description and code, that you want to use, or click "generate random code" to get automatic result.

Press on "Conditions" and enter total quantity available and available quantity for each user.

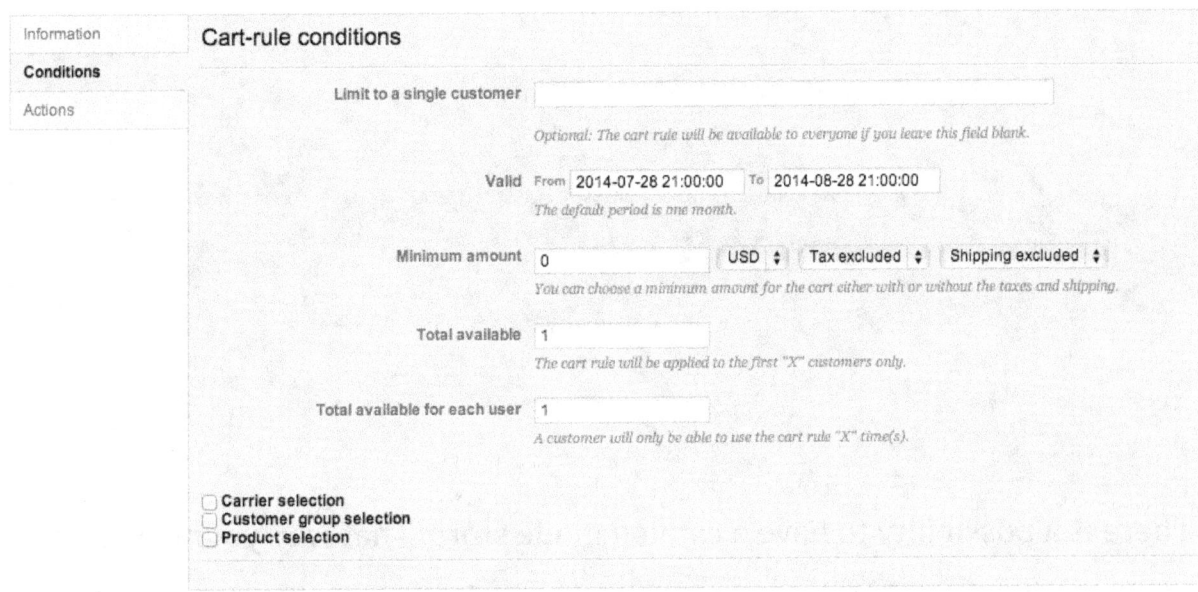

Open tab "Actions" and choose which discount you want to use: free shipping, percentage from total sum or amount of a discount.

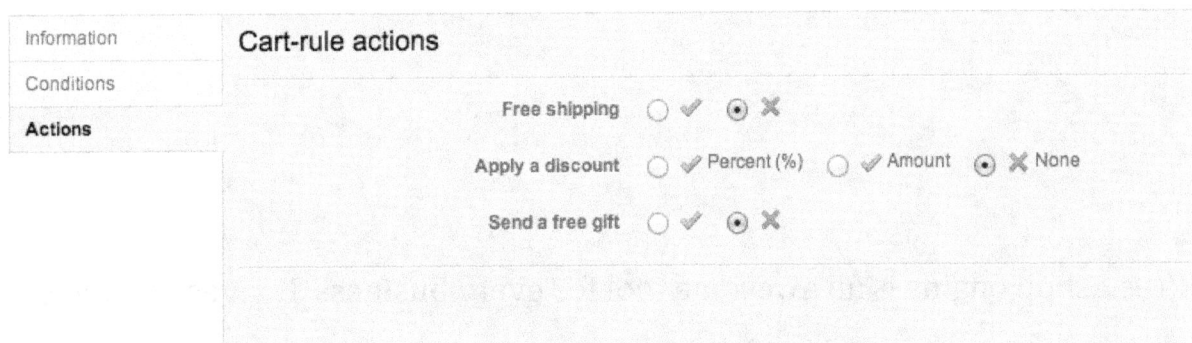

For example, let's enter 20% and press "Save". Now your customers, who enter this code at the checkout, will automatically receive 20% discount.

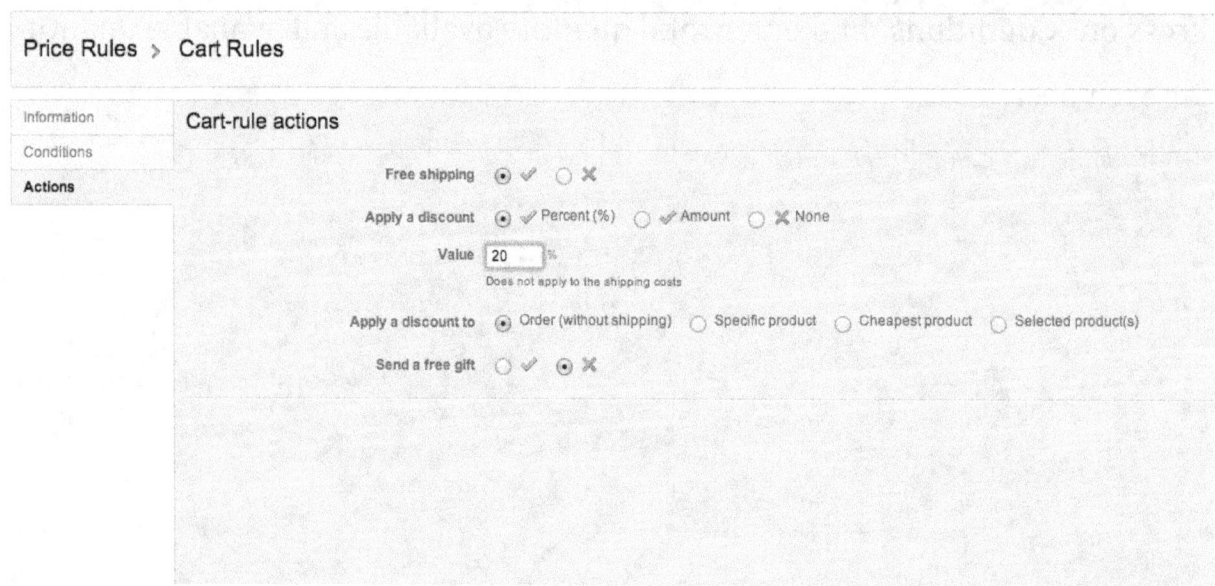

There is a possibility to have a catalog mode store. That way your customers can't purchase anything, they can only see products you offer. In order to use this mode, open "Preferences"-> "Products" and choose catalog mode. Press "Save".

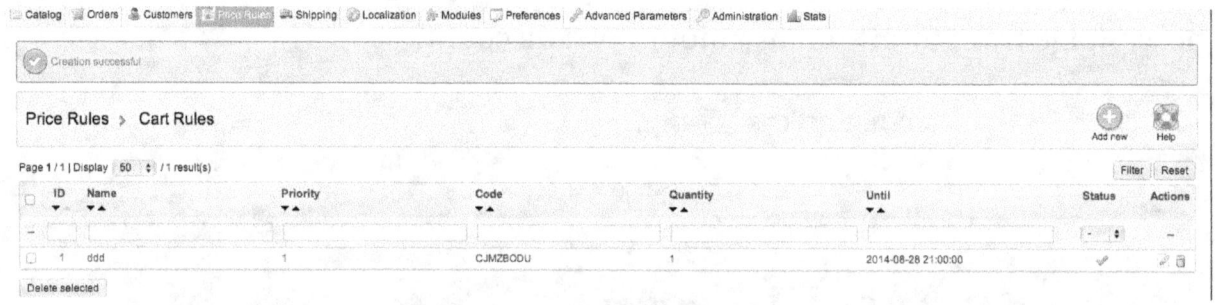

Prestashop engine is an awesome tool for every business. It gives you the best tools to run a successful business without spending extra money for merchandizing solutions.

9
MODULES

One of the most important things in prostashop is a module. I can even say that, whole online store built in prestashop depends on modules. In prestashop modules are used in every part of your store. Each module can be positioned in a specific location. In this chapter I will explain how modules can be installed, positioned and used. I will give you examples and show you how to set up specific modules into your store. However, at first, let me explain what modules are in prestashop.

Modules control each separate part of your online store in prestashop. For example, you have a picture slider on your homepage - it is controlled by picture slider module. You have a manufacturers' slider or new products slider, they are controlled by special modules as well. Even your shopping cart has a separate module. There are social networks-modules, sharing buttons-modules and etc. So, every time you want to add some extra function for your store, you, basically, will add a module and point its position where you want it.

Prestashop comes with a handy list of modules already preprogrammed into its marketplace. The most important modules are available for installation for free. Some of the most needed modules will be automatically installed with your prestashop, others are optional and can be installed by you. In case a module is not available through the marketplace, you can always install it manually. However, let's try installing module from the marketplace first.

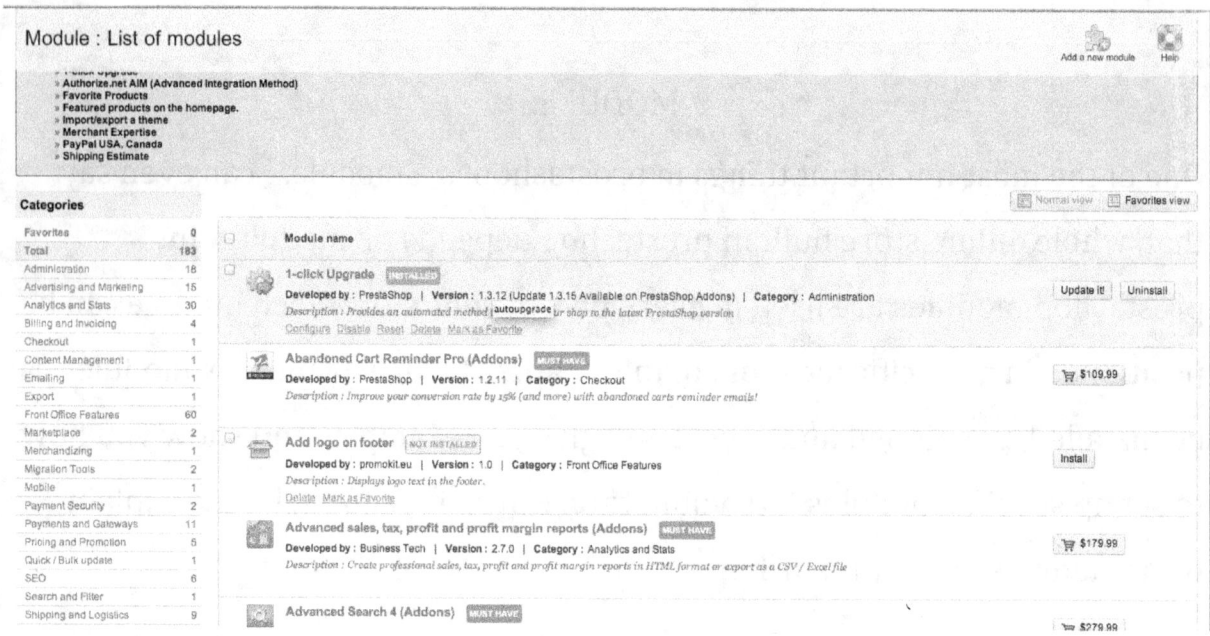

You can also see, if a module is already installed.

In order to install any specific module, you need to open "Module" and locate this module in your prestashop marketplace. For example, I will install "Block contact info" for my footer.

Press "Install" on the right. After installation is complete enter your contact information and press "Update settings".

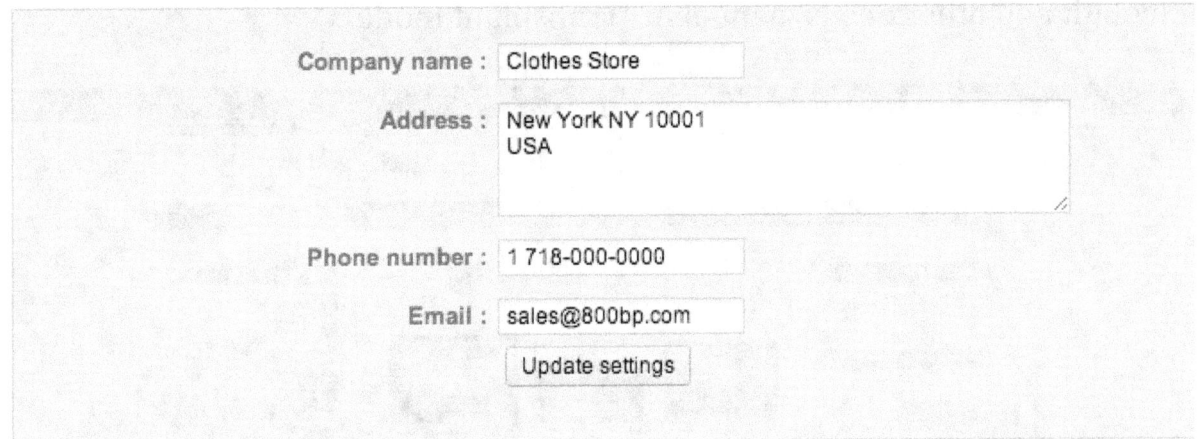

Your module is successfully installed and your customers can easily find you.

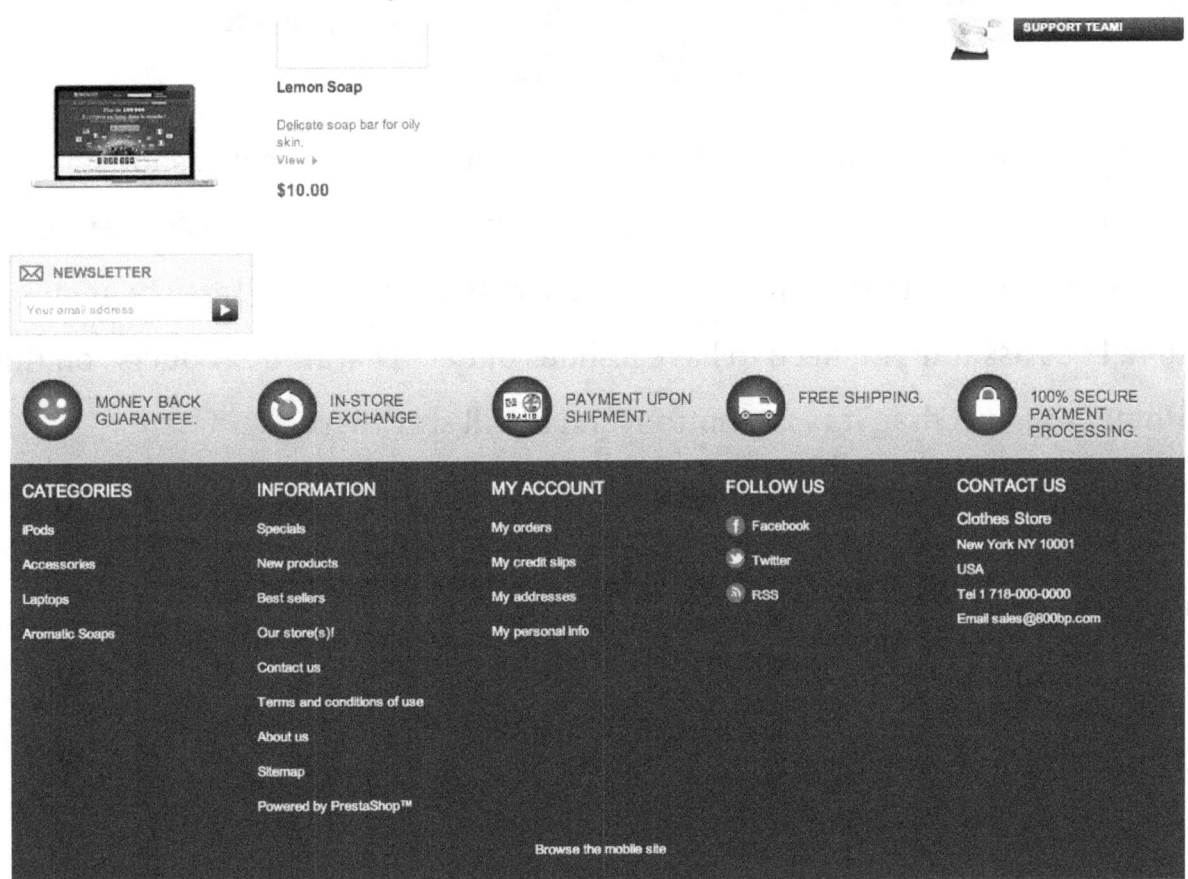

Open "Modules"-> "Positions". There are 2 ways to change position of your modules in your store. First one is an automatic drag and drop through LiveEdit and other one is manual in "Transplant mode".

Let's try to position your module with LiveEdit. Each part that is shown in highlighted border is controlled by separate module. You can just drag it to the part you wish it to be displayed, or delete it by pressing a trash bean next to it. Let's assume you need to have a slider under "Featured products" on the Homepage. Just drag it to the bottom and it will stay there.

Make sure you press "Save" LiveEdit when you've finished.

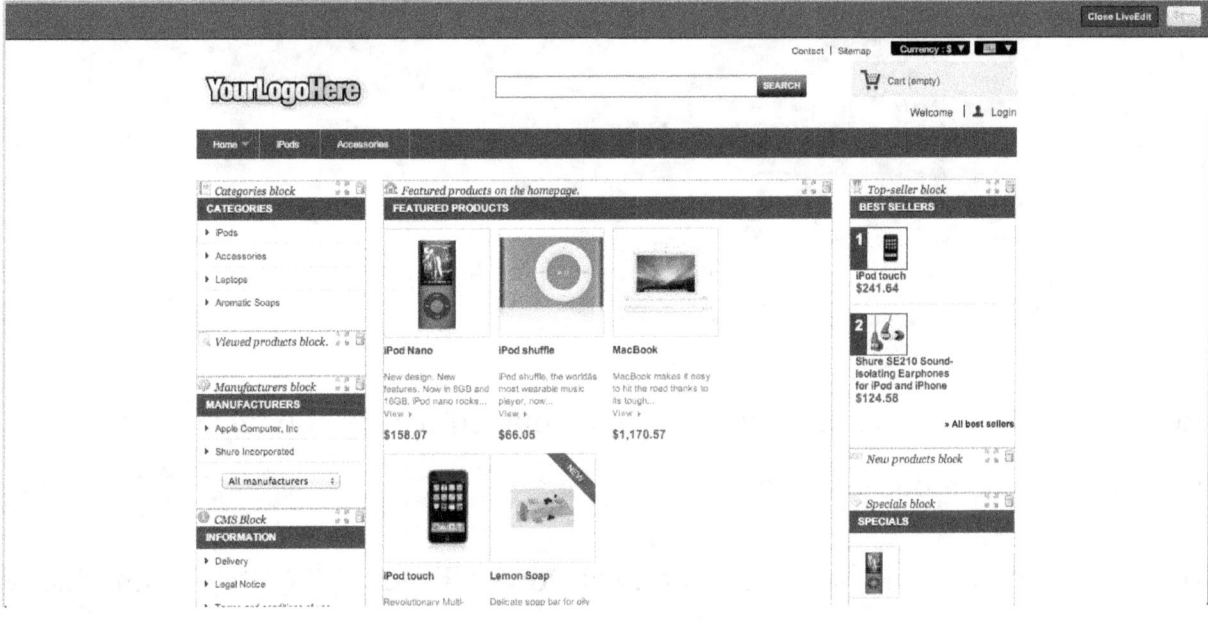

You can always position modules manually by choosing "Transplant a module".

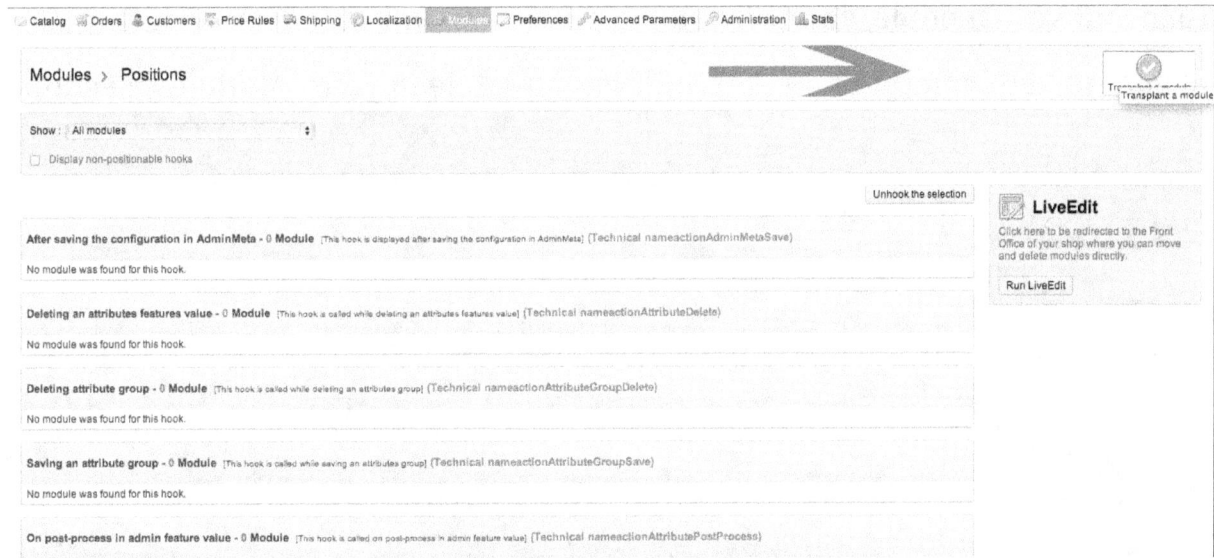

This function is very useful in the situation, when you have installed a custom template. Just choose a module from the list and hook it to the location, where you want it to be displayed.

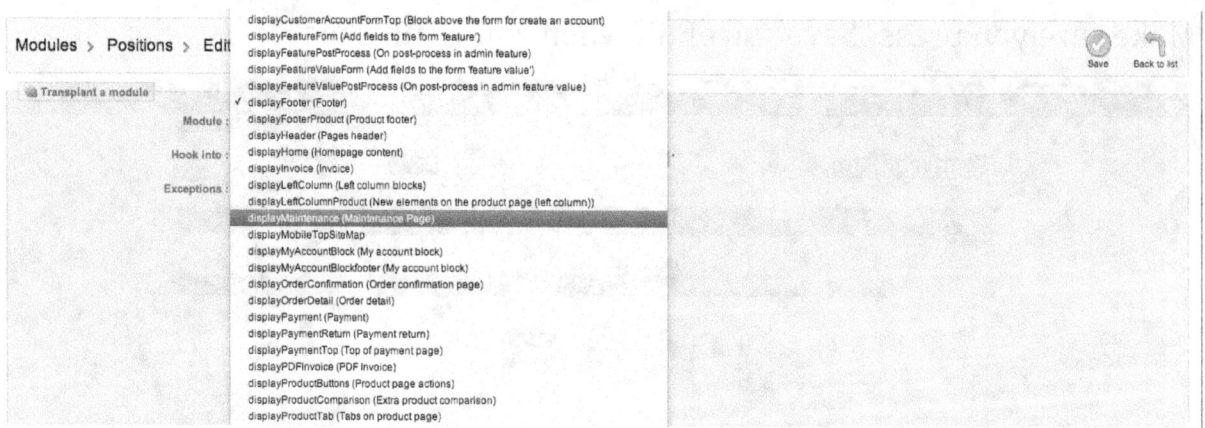

Remember, that not all modules can be displayed where you wish. It all depends on the module options.

Usually, when module has some changes, you will see an update automatically available for installation. Just press on this and your module will be updated. However, make sure your setup options didn't change after the update.

Let's see a situation when module is not available in the marketplace. In order to install such module, you will need to download and save this module in Zip format to your computer. Press "Add New" module in your "Modules" section.

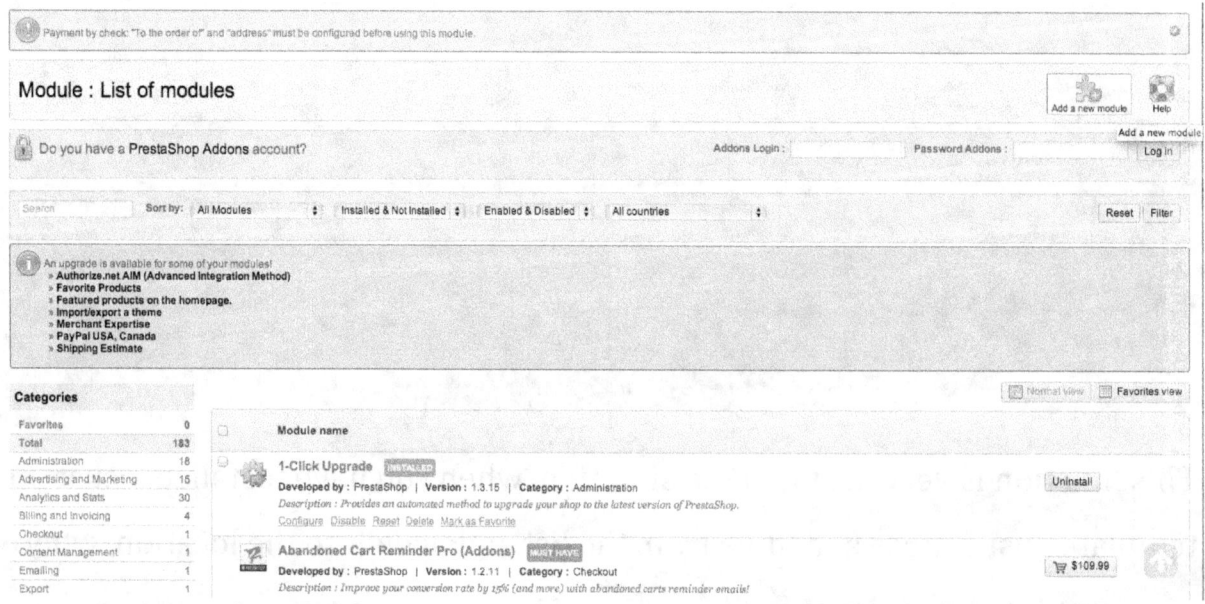

Select module from your computer and press "Upload". When this module is uploaded, prestashop will automatically point you to it.

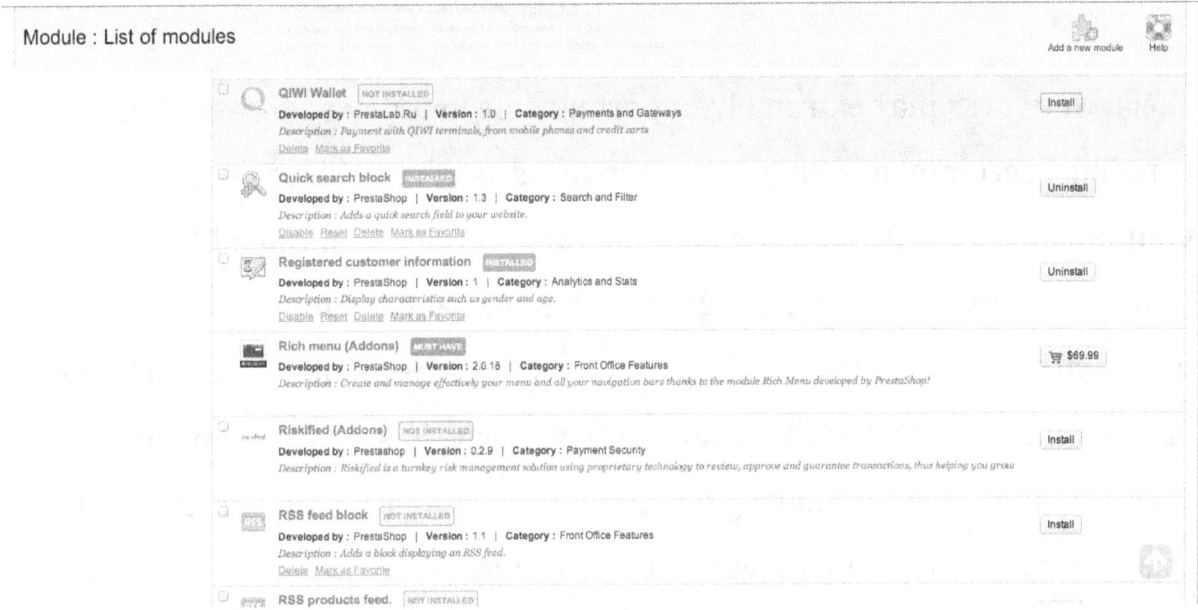

Now you can press "Install", enter your specific data, needed for this module, and start using it.

It's easy as one-two-three, when you have everything what is needed.

Please note! Lots of templates come with already preloaded modules for a specific template. In that case, to change a template configuration and look, you need to edit modules that come with it.

Most templates come with instruction manuals. Try to setup everything according to the instruction and your store will be working perfectly. Make sure to always rearrange thumbnails when changing size of your pictures.

10
SOCIAL NETWORKS IMPLEMENTATION

Social Networks play extremely important role in today's successful business running. I recommend using social networks as advertising campaigns for your business. Create Facebook and Twitter account. You can add Sharing buttons to your store and start getting response and feedback from your potential customers. Announce special deals and discounts, for example for Facebook users, and see the response right away. It is easy to implement "Facebook like box" or Sharing buttons into your store. I recommend doing this. Since many customers who liked a product you're selling, would also like to share it with their friends or loved ones, to ask their opinion before buying it.

In order to do this you just need to download "Facebook like box" module and install it for your store.

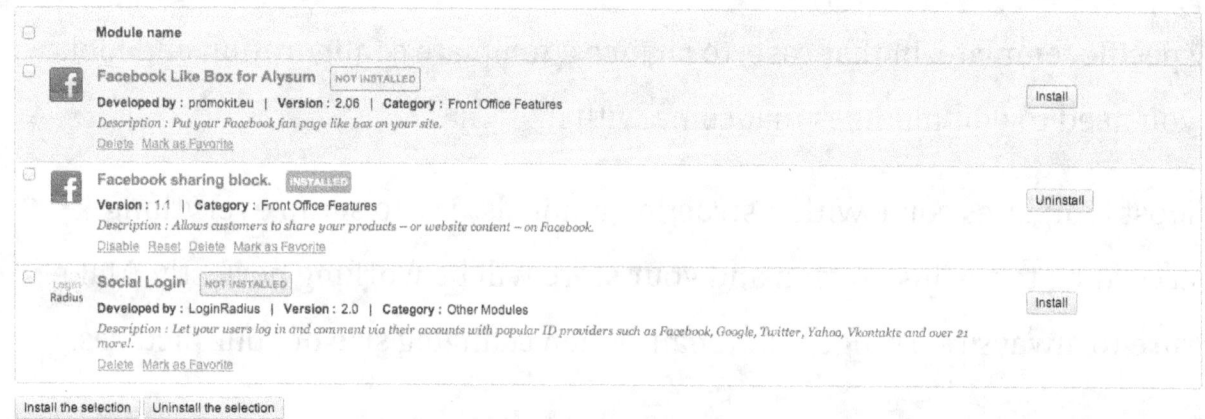

Most of the modern templates come with this module already preinstalled. All you need is, just enter your Facebook address and it is ready to use.

I also recommend installing Sharing buttons for your store. It is an easy and convenient way to have your customers share products you sell.

On your Facebook account you can always promote your store and your products for specific locations and it will not cost you a fortune. As of today, social networks are one of the most popular and convenient ways to promote your products or your store.

You can also use other social networks for product promotion. Twitter would give you some great results as well. I want to pay special attention to Blogs. Create one simple and easy to read blog on a popular engine, like Tumblr, Blogger or Livejournal. Start advertising products and ideas, start posting interesting facts and promotions there. You will gain lots of followers. Make sure you include your main store link in every post you do. That way, your store will start getting lots of attention from your users and will start to get popularity on the internet. Once you create your blog, start building relationship with your customers. Start giving them opportunities to buy something cheaper, than it is sold in your store. Introduce yourself as a big company, willing to care about your customers. If you get any complaints, try to handle them on a side. Ask email address of that customer and try to satisfy him via email. If you share interesting feeds with your social networks, it can spread extremely fast and easily increase your visibility with new leads. Join different communities and groups on Facebook and post about your products there. That way you will get more visibility as well. Moreover, before doing all that, make sure your Facebook page have more than 30 likes and the web address is easily accessible and easy to remember for others. Try to post often. At the beginning try to post mostly informational content, not promotions, as this will gain more trust from your customers.

Besides, you can use "YouTube" for your store promotions. Create your channel, post interesting videos and include links to your store or your products in the videos.

Nowadays social networks are extremely important to run a successful business. More and more people use them every day for business and pleasure. Use this opportunity to gain more customers. Use social networks for advertisings and you will have visible results very soon.

11

STATISTICS AND EMPLOYEE MANAGEMENT

In Prestashop you have an ability to add and delete your employees.

For example, when you have a store and you have several employees, you can create separate access for each of them. You can also give some rights to manage your store for one employee and remove some rights from another.

Open tab "Administration" and choose "Employees"

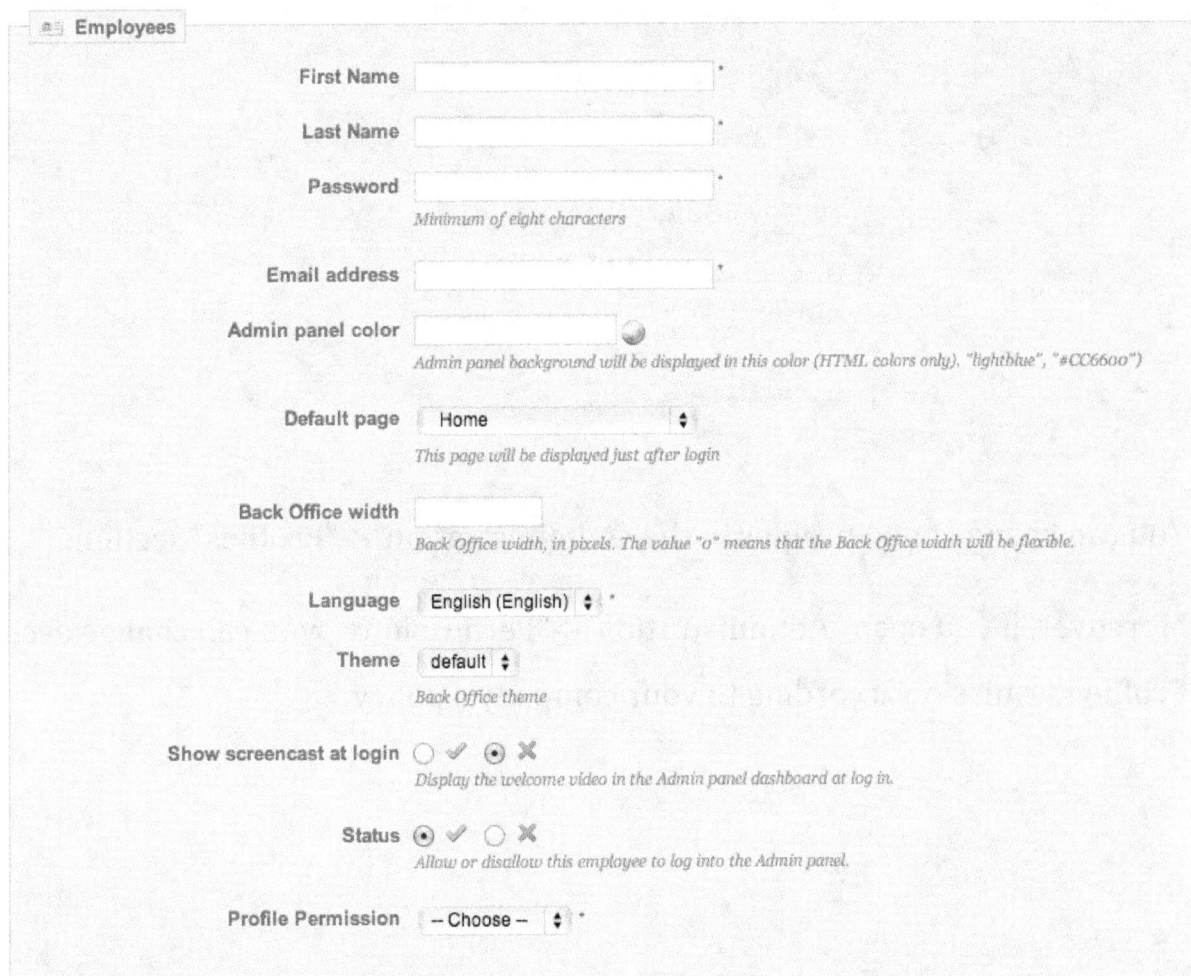

Press "Add New", and enter all necessary information.

Choose Profile Permission and press "Save".

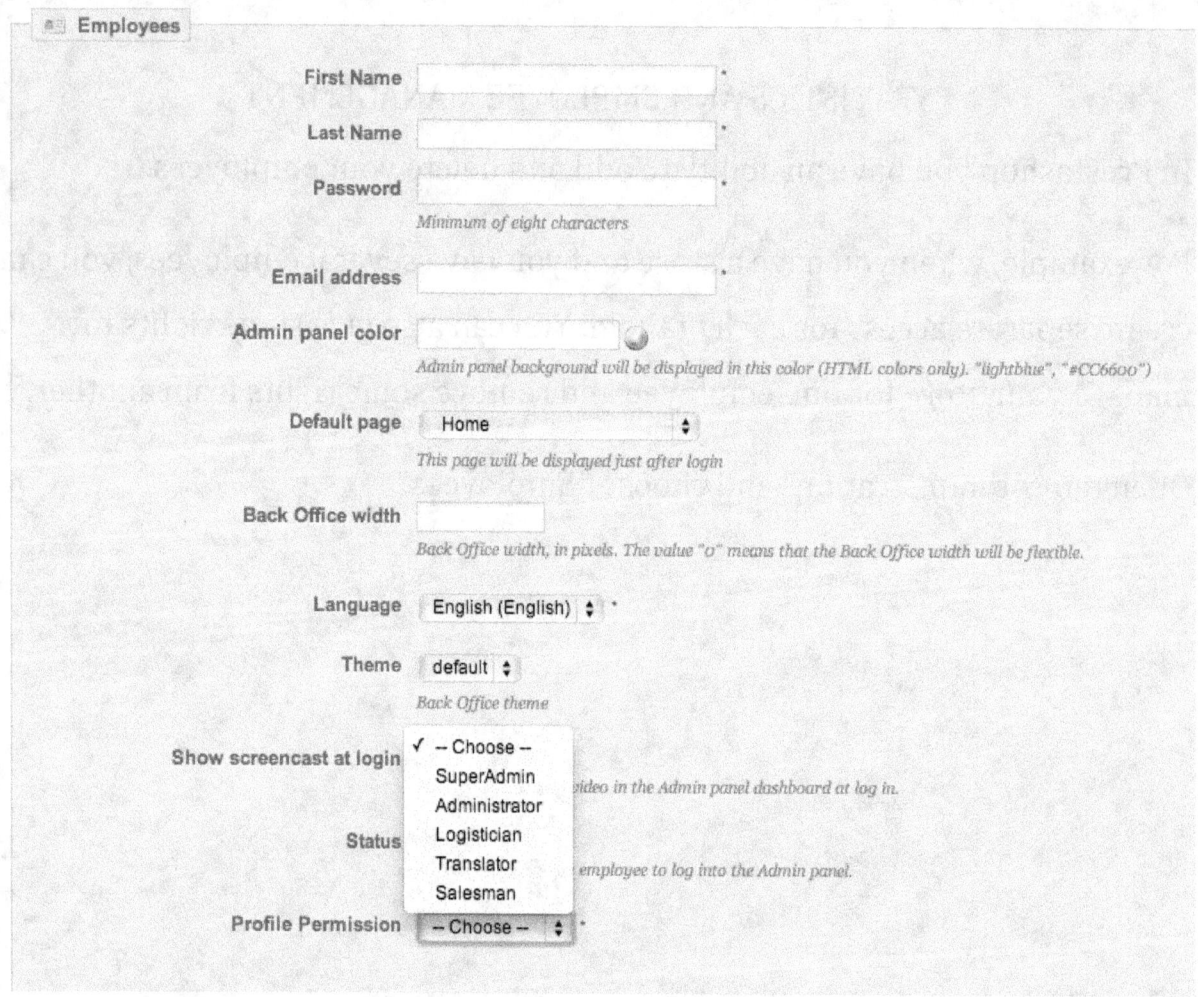

You can change or ad profiles in the "Administration"->"Profiles" section.

Moreover, if you open "Administration"->"Permissions", you can change each Profile Permission according to your company's policy.

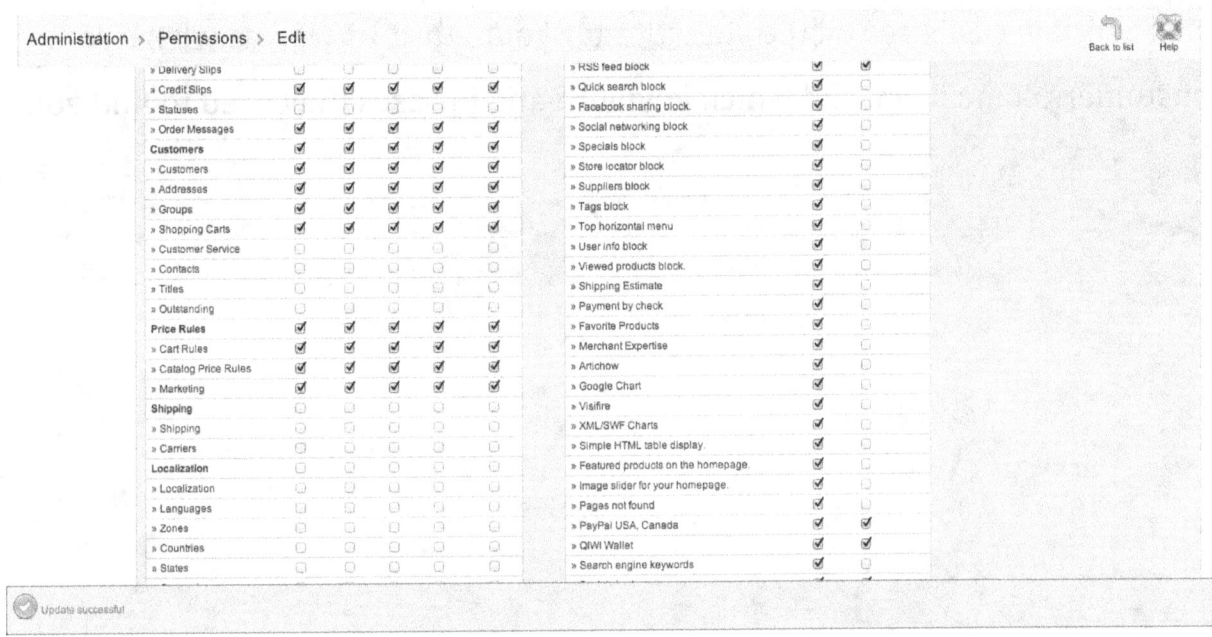

For example, if you want your salesperson to be able to change or add discounts, just select salesperson on the left and select his rights from the list.

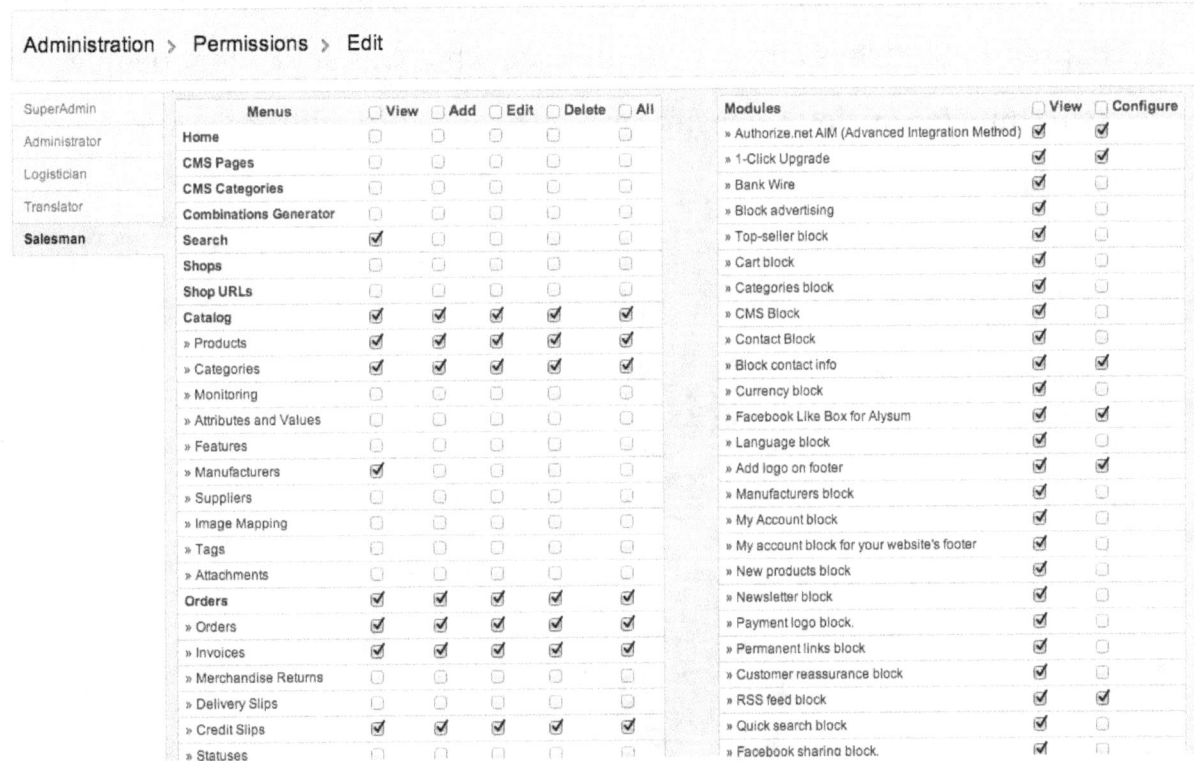

You can also easily see all the statistics for your store, as well as where your customers come from, and which keyword and phrases they used to find you.

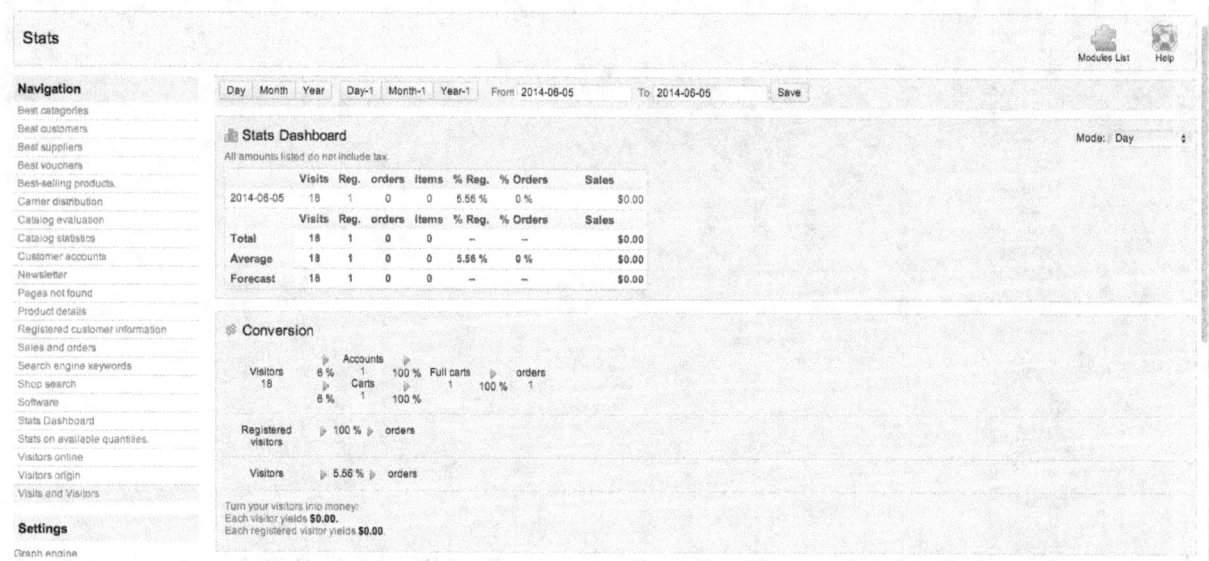

It is extremely important for every business to know those phrases and use them for future website optimization. I will explain more about that in our SEO chapter. In Statistics tab you can also see what was sold, what people were searching for on your website, as well as latest IP addresses and software they used.

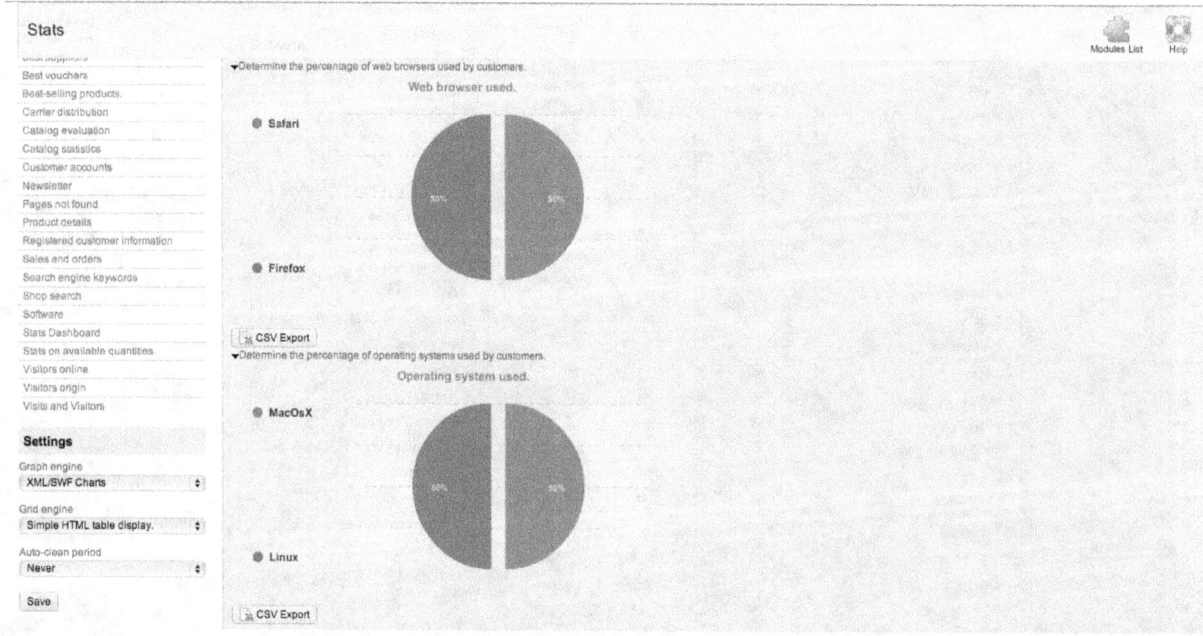

Statistics navigation gives you full ability to monitor all the aspects of your online store and business running.

Now, when your store is working properly and ready to earn you money, let's learn how to make your store visible for everyone. Business will not run successfully without monitoring.

12

SEO FOR YOUR STORE

The store will not work properly, if customers never hear about it. SEO is one of the most important factors for successful business running.

Search Engine Optimization (SEO) is the process of affecting the visibility of a website in search engines natural or unpaid organic search results (ref: wikipedia.com). Every online store has to be visible for everyone. Then more people see your website, the more sales you will likely have. Keywords play a very important factor in successful search engine visibility. Before choosing keywords, you need to understand, what main product you are trying to sell. Then you need to write down main keywords for exact products. Find those products online and see what keywords are used by other stores to describe this product. Use similar synonyms to describe your products. When adding synonyms, try not to use lots of words that are not related to specific products and don't use keywords that are too specific for your area or town. Use brand names in your keywords as well.

Your Homepage content plays a very important role in your websites' global visibility. You need to be sure to add the most important keywords and phrases to your Homepage. Add most popular products and brands to your Homepage. Be sure your Homepage have enough text information.

Your product's descriptions have to be short, but detailed. It needs to have all the important features of your product, but not exceed ten lines. Do not copy the content from your suppliers, as search engines don't like doubled contents. It is also recommended to use unique product names.

Tags of the products have to be around 100 to 150 characters. In Prestashop you can add tags to every product.

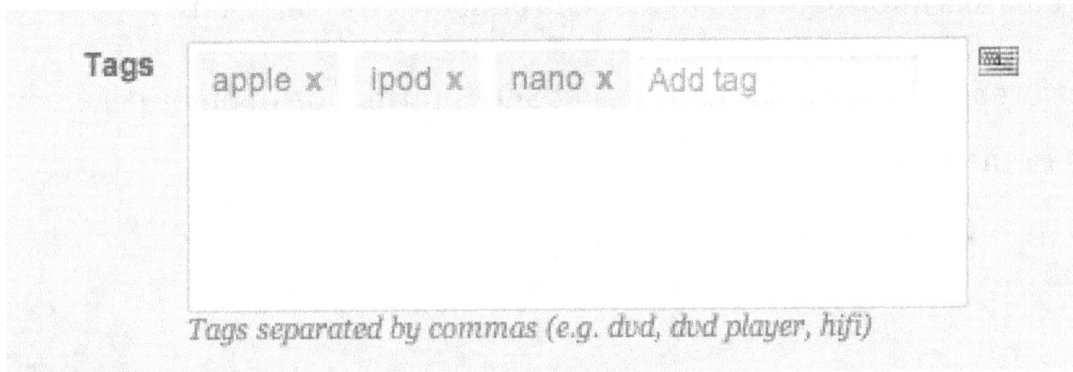

Open your product to edit and add tags in the "Information" tab. Open "Catalog" - "Products" – "SEO" tab and add title, description and keywords for each specific product.

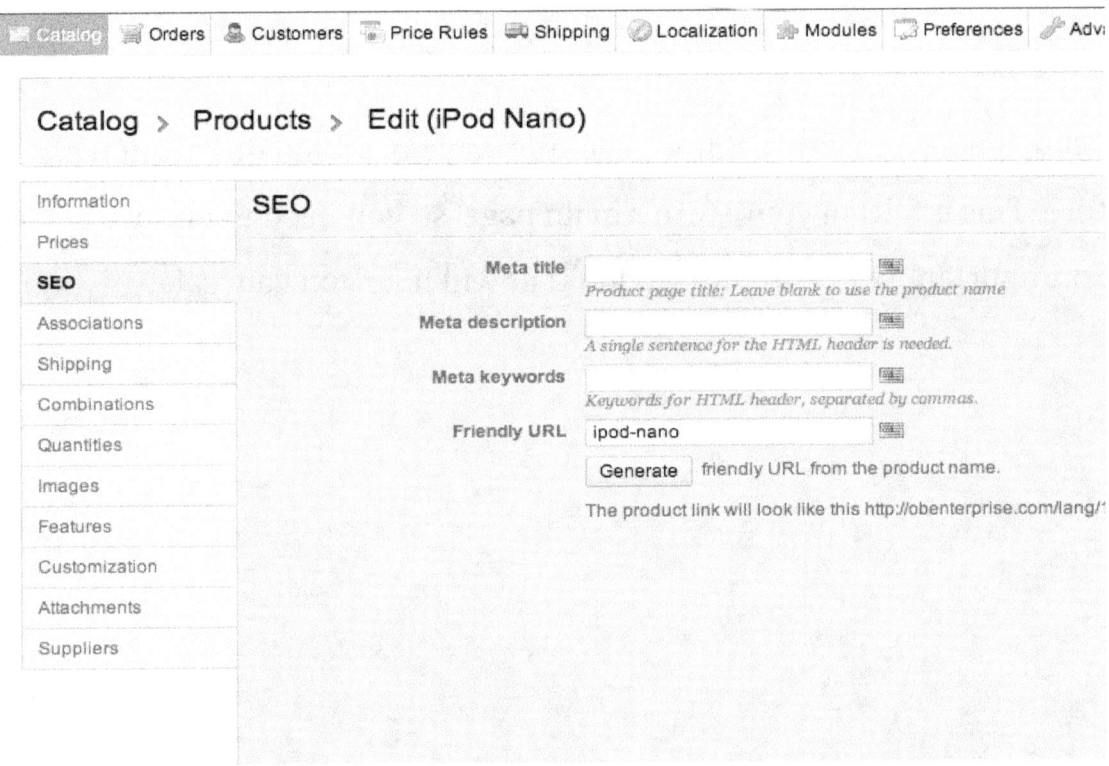

Press "Save" and it's ready to use. If you have many products in your store, there are several helpful modules available in Prestashop which give you ability to edit this information in bulk (all products at the same time).

Open "Preferences"-> "SEO & URLs" to edit SEO information of other pages, including Homepage.

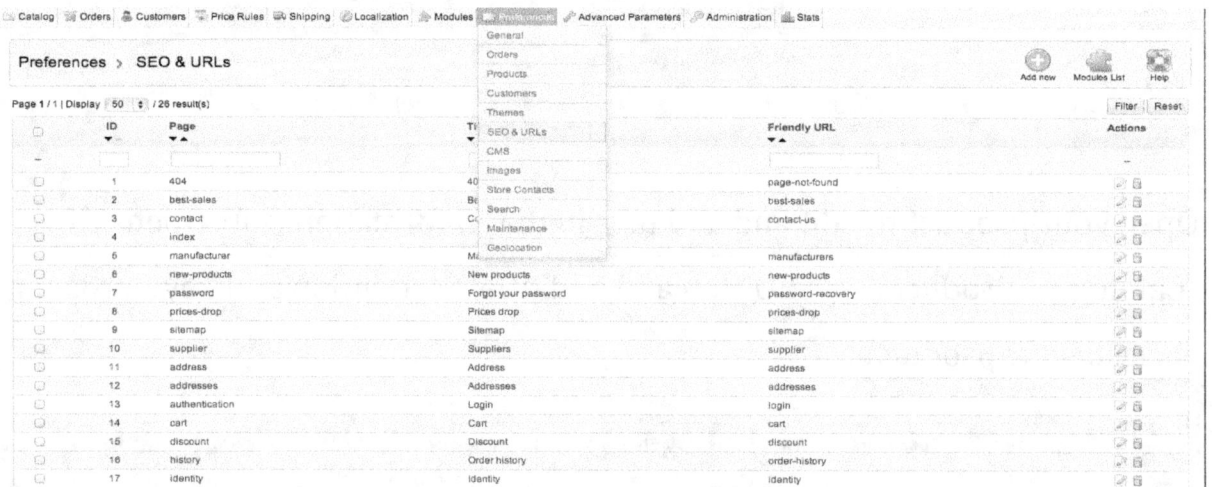

Select Edit icon next to index. Enter page title, keywords and description of your store. This is SEO of your store's main page, so you need to be sure to use the most important words in this section that will help you gain sales.

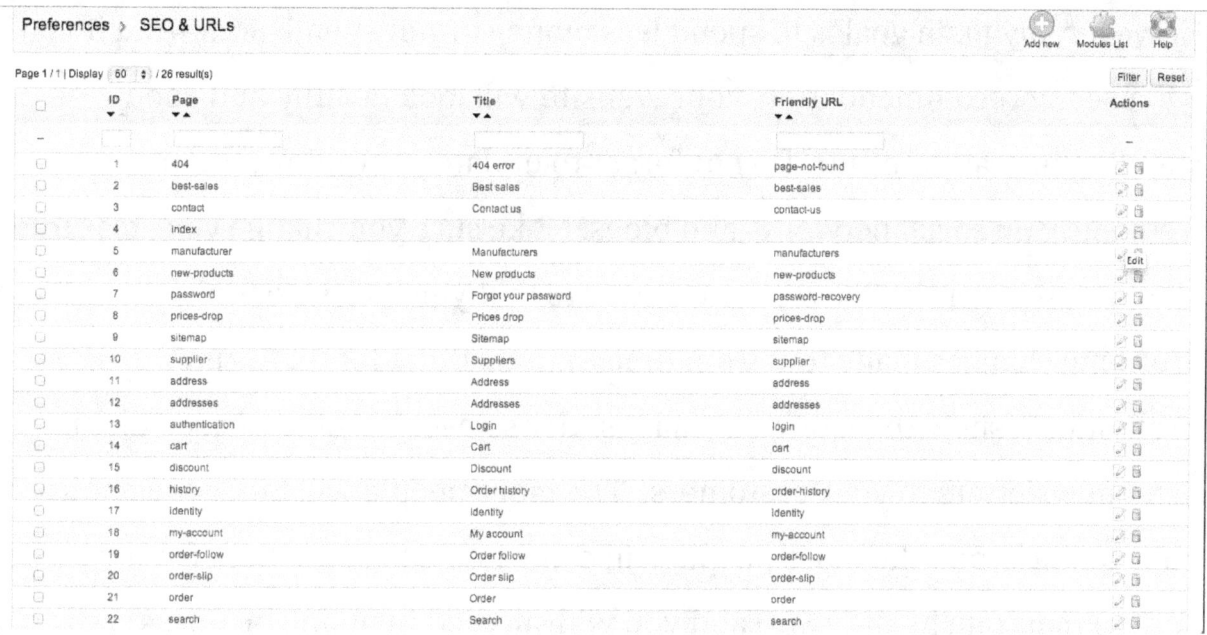

Press "Save" and your store is live and ready to bring you money.

I also recommend installing a "Sitemap" module.

Now, the most important thing in all SEO is to let "Google" know that your website exists. Go to google.com/webmastertools and open a free account there.

Add your website to that account. Use one of the methods to confirm ownership of the website. After you have done those steps, upload your website sitemap, and ask "Google" to crawl and index your website. Now your web store is absolutely visible and your customers can easily find you online.

All those recommendation cannot guarantee good results, but those are the only free ways that I recommend to make your website visible and successful. You can also edit other pages' SEO information in "SEO & URLs" section. The more pages you edit, the more your website will be visible to others. There is always another way to make your website popup in front of the search results.

However, my main goal is to spend less money or not spend at all. And if you will use my recommendation, your website will look healthy and good standing in search results. Do not forget to update your information frequently on social networks and blogs. Make sure you change your featured products frequently. Show your customers that your website is alive and there are some changes made to it from time to time. Don't forget to run promotions, show them on your main slider so every visitor can see them. Send newsletters to your customers. The more people will talk good about your online store, the more people will come and buy something from you. Be sure to maintain healthy SEO and you will succeed in online business.

13
FINAL TOUCH UPS AND UPGRADES

Online store is one of the most convenient ways to purchase products from the comfort of your home, no need to spend time (and money) to travel, to search all over for local shops that sell necessary products, to look for a place to park, to spend hours in public transport or to stand in long lines at the supermarket. E-commerce solutions are our future.

Prestashop is one of them.

5.6

The design of a newer version 5.6 is slightly different, but all functions are absolutely the same. Here is an example of how it looks and where all the important buttons are located.

Front Office

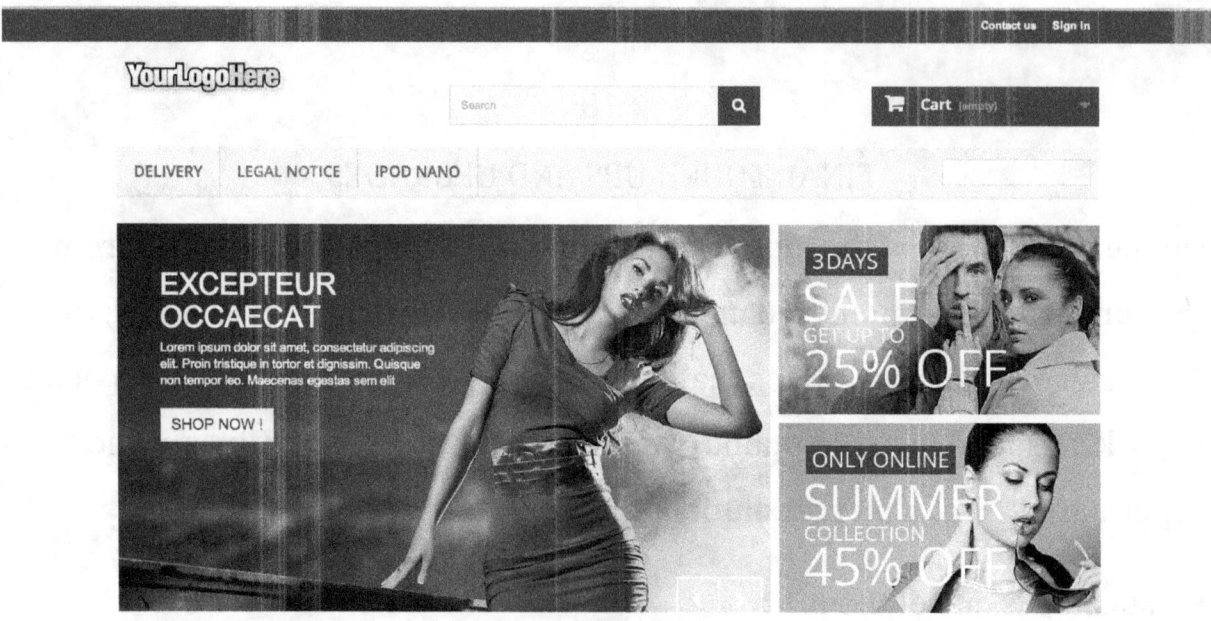

Back Office

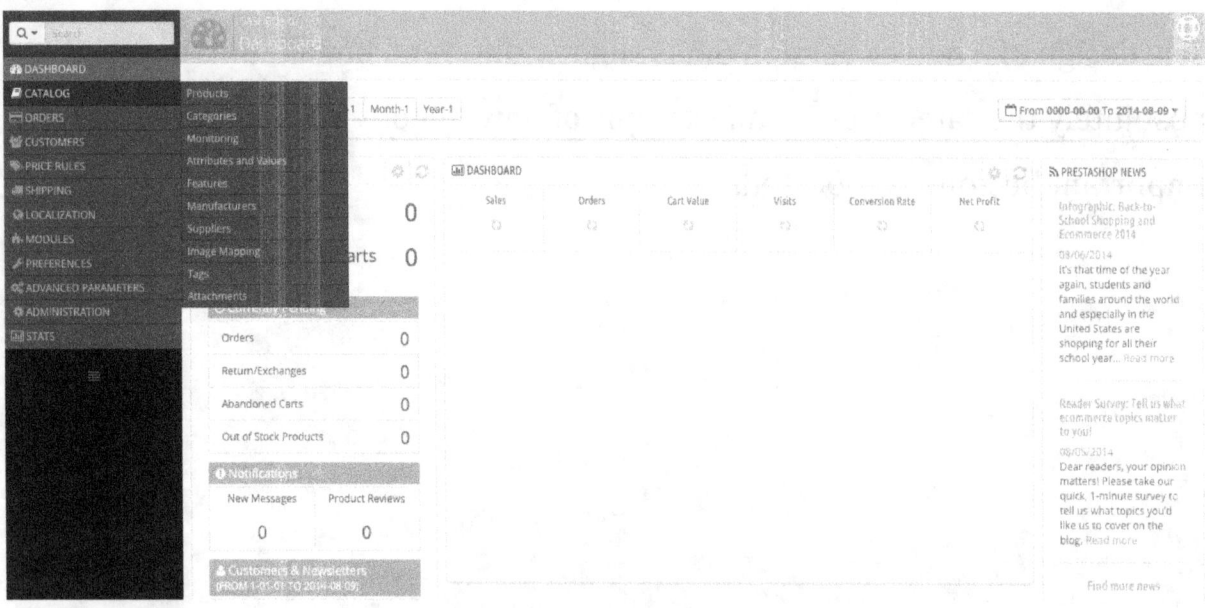

Add Product page

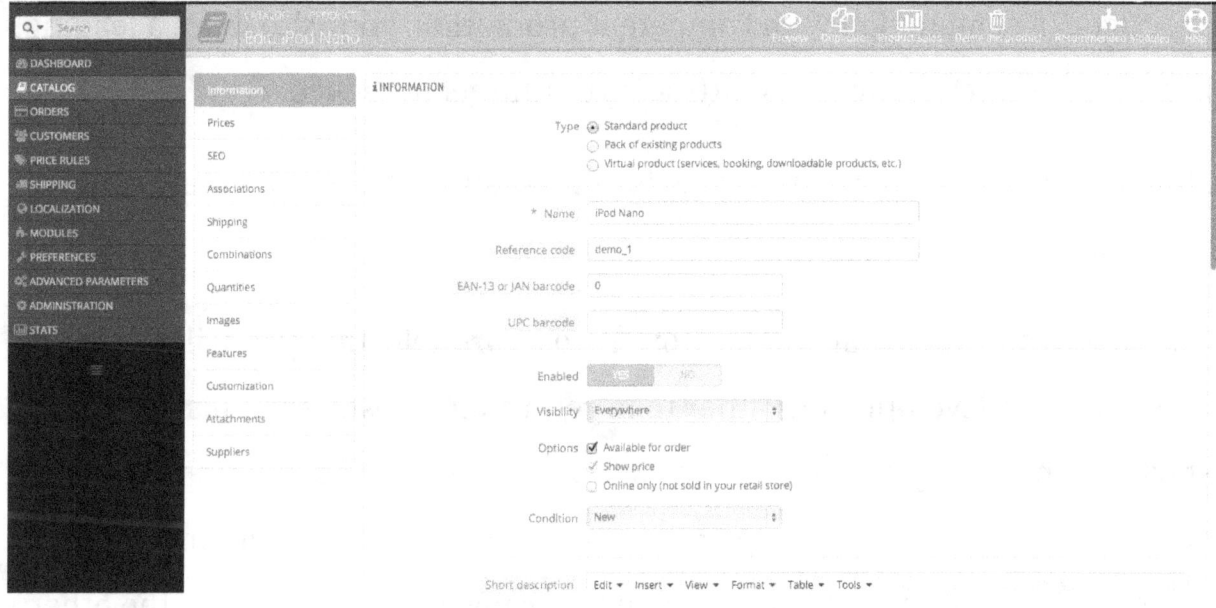

Save Button

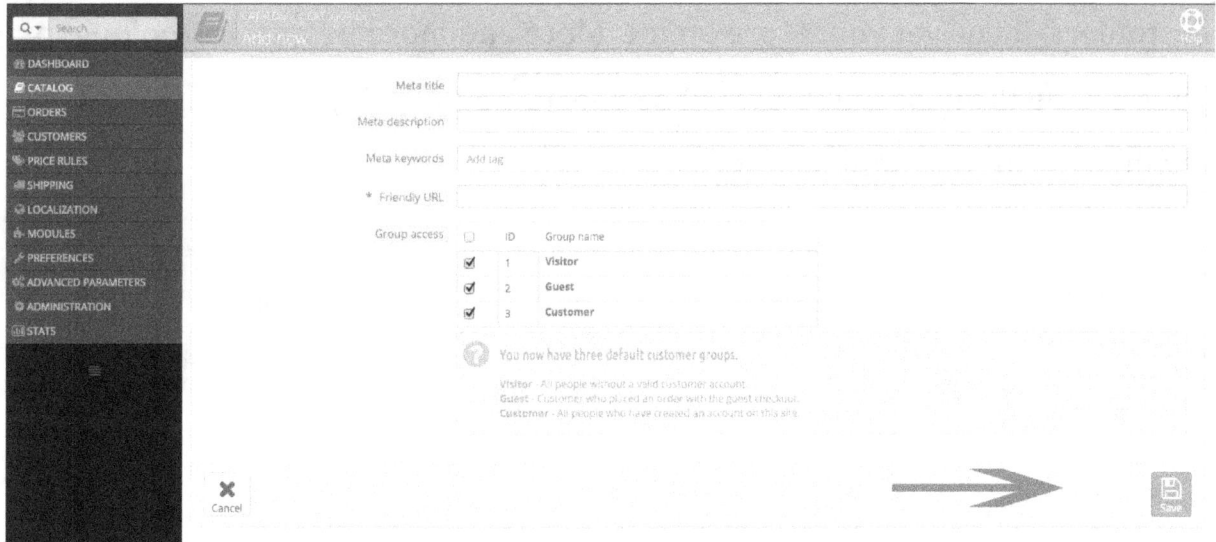

All setup and functions can be edited the same way as in previous versions.

Thoughtful and convenient interface makes it easy to purchase. People are returning to where they feel comfortable. Satisfied customer will become your regular customer and would recommend the project to his/her friends.

Fast loading pages and optimized codes accelerate the indexing of new products. In conjunction with competent promotion, your site takes a leading position in search engines and attracts your target audience.

Simple administration reduces time for processing orders and entering new information into the database.

The cost of developing an online store is so affordable, that you will think about project development, rather than return on investment, plus you can start making money as soon as you have your store up and running. From one side, it doesn't require you to pay rent every month or pay your employees' salaries (you can run this store by yourself from your house). From the other end, if you already have a physical store, you will have much more sales and customers, if you get your store online. More and more people are looking for your products online and they will be able to find you, if you use my techniques and recommendations.

Good Luck!

REFERENCES

1. Prestashop CMS and website
2. Online research
3. http://www.wikipedia.org/

2014

New York, USA

www.ingramcontent.com/pod-product-compliance
Lightning Source LLC
Chambersburg PA
CBHW080948170526
45158CB00008B/2409